Power in Weakness

THE NEW TESTAMENT IN CONTEXT

Friendship and Finances in Philippi
THE LETTER OF PAUL TO THE PHILIPPIANS
Ben Witherington III

Walking in the Truth: Perseverers and Deserters
THE FIRST, SECOND, AND THIRD LETTERS OF JOHN
Gerard S. Sloyan

Church and Community in Crisis
THE GOSPEL ACCORDING TO MATTHEW
J. Andrew Overman

Letters to Paul's Delegates
1 TIMOTHY, 2 TIMOTHY, TITUS
Luke Timothy Johnson

Embassy of Onesimus
THE LETTER OF PAUL TO PHILEMON
Allen Dwight Callahan

Community of the Wise
THE LETTER OF JAMES
Robert W. Wall

To Every Nation under Heaven
THE ACTS OF THE APOSTLES
Howard Clark Kee

Fallen Is Babylon
THE REVELATION TO JOHN
Frederick J. Murphy

Power in Weakness
CONFLICT AND RHETORIC IN PAUL'S
SECOND LETTER TO THE CORINTHIANS
Sze-kar Wan

Power in Weakness

CONFLICT AND RHETORIC IN PAUL'S SECOND LETTER TO THE CORINTHIANS

Sze-kar Wan

THE NEW TESTAMENT IN CONTEXT

Howard Clark Kee and J. Andrew Overman, editors

TRINITY PRESS INTERNATIONAL

Harrisburg, Pennsylvania

Trinity Press International, P.O. Box 1321, Harrisburg, PA 17105
Trinity Press International is a division of the Morehouse Group

Library of Congress Cataloging-in-Publication Data

Wan, Sze-kar.
    Power in weakness : conflict and rhetoric in Paul's Second letter to the Corinthians / Sze-kar Wan.
        p.   cm. — (New Testament in context)
    Includes bibliographical references.
    ISBN 1-56338-315-2 (pbk. : alk. paper)
    1. Bible. N.T. Corinthians, 2nd – Criticism, interpretation, etc.   I. Title.
II. Series.

BS2675.2 .W36   2000
227'.307 –dc21
                                                                      99-087136

Printed in the United States of America

00   01   02   03   04   05   10   9   8   7   6   5   4   3   2   1

Contents

Chapter One

Introduction

Sherlock Holmes said to Watson, "The ring, man, the ring: that was what he came back for. If we have no other way of catching him, we can always bait our line with the ring. . . . [This is] the finest study I ever came across: a study in scarlet, eh? Why shouldn't we use a little art jargon. There's the scarlet thread of murder running through the colourless skein of life, and our study is to unravel it, and isolate it, and expose every inch of it."

—Arthur Conan Doyle

Second Corinthians ranks as one of the most challenging of Paul's letters for the biblical detective to unravel. Reasons for this difficulty are manifold, not the least of which is the formidable task of needing to reconstruct the entire exchange between Paul and the Corinthians before one could say anything positive about the letter. What dooms such an enterprise from the start is, of course, the unhappy fact that we have in 2 Corinthians a one-sided, even biased, representation of the whole picture. Reading Paul's letters is always akin to listening in on a heated phone conversation while hearing only one side of it: we can make out what Paul is saying with reasonable certainty, but detective work and a healthy dosage of informed imagination will have to fill in the rest of the picture. What, for example, might have prompted the puzzling exchanges — much of it now lost to us — between Paul and his converts? How did the other side respond to Paul's sometimes conciliatory, sometimes angry rhetoric? What was the relationship between Paul and his congregation? Nevertheless, as tedious as this problem is, this is by no means a unique problem in Pauline studies. Readers of any of Paul's letters are faced with the same prospect of reconstructing events presupposed by and reflected in the text, and reading

2 Corinthians is no different. This reason by itself would not make interpreting 2 Corinthians the daunting task that it is.

What makes reconstructing the dialogue between Paul and his interlocutors doubly difficulty, however, is that we encounter in 2 Corinthians not a dispassionate conversation between disinterested parties but a polemical Paul, whom we would least expect to give us unbiased information about his opponents. When, for example, he suggests to the Corinthian congregation that they forgive the person who has grievously offended him (2:6–8; 7:12), is this meant ironically or literally? Is this statement a basis firm enough to reconstruct the shadowy events behind it? We are faced with the same uncertainty when Paul, in full polemical flight, fires off a long string of interjections supposedly to counter his opponents' boastful claims in what he calls a "fool's speech":

> Are they Hebrews? So am I. Are they Israelites? So am I. Are they seed of Abraham? So am I. Are they ministers of Christ? —I am speaking like a madman—I am more: with more labors, with more prisons, with far more blows, often near death. Five times I received from the Jews forty strokes minus one, three times I was beaten with a rod, once I was stoned, three times I have been shipwrecked, for a night and day I was in the depths of water; often on journeys, in dangers from rivers, in dangers from robbers, in dangers from kinsfolk, in dangers from the gentiles, in dangers in cities, in dangers in the wilderness, in dangers at sea, in dangers among false brothers; in labor and hardship, in wakefulness often, in hunger and in thirst, often without food, in coldness and nakedness; not to mention the pressure on me every day, from anxiety for all the churches (11:22–28).

Who exactly were these "Hebrews" and "Israelites" who also turned out to be "ministers of Christ"? What was Paul's issue with them? Paul's description of presumably the same group of people elsewhere in 11:15 is even less helpful: surely Paul does not mean that they are literally "Satan's ministers"! Is all this an exaggeration, or is there a sure way to lift the polemical veil to uncover the debate responsible for it?

These are legitimate questions, but the problem of deciphering Paul's polemics is not unique to 2 Corinthians. We have come to expect Paul's spontaneity, impetuosity, outbursts, passionate prose, hyperboles, and other querulous comments of similar nature. Scholars in generations past, as a matter of fact, were so conditioned by this view of Paul that they thought his whole theology had been incubated in a disputatious culture. They pointed to Paul's confrontation with Peter in Antioch (Gal 2:11–14) as the starting point of that trend which finally culminated in the separation of gentile and Jewish Christianity. Even though today we might dismiss this rather one-sided interpretation for not giving enough weight to Paul's more irenic compositions elsewhere,[1] Paul's contentious reputation has become firmly fixed. Second Corinthians, of course, does nothing to dislodge it from our collective memory.

What renders 2 Corinthians truly unusual, if not in fact unique, in the Pauline corpus, indeed in the whole New Testament, is the preponderance of jarringly disjointed arguments and narratives throughout the letter. Even if we make allowance for Paul's penchant for abrupt changes in topics, his stop-and-go prose, and his mind-bending U-turns in thoughts, it is still difficult to account for what we find in 2 Corinthians. For example, after Paul has just concluded a plea for leniency on behalf of an offending member in the Corinthian church (2:5–11) and before he could finish narrating his travel plans from Troas to Macedonia (2:12–13), the text begins a long, complicated discourse loosely based on the story of Moses' veil as recounted in the book of Exodus (2:14–5:21). In this section Paul tantalizes us with hints about some unknown opponents who were evidently none other than his fellow-missionaries. We can infer from his polemics that these critics must have leveled some charges against him — whether implicitly or openly, we do not know. But unfortunately for us Paul does not address his opponents directly or defend his mission explicitly; he seems content with a long discourse on the meaning of ministry. An authentic ministry is characterized by weakness and humility, so that the power of God can be manifested. It is also at bottom a ministry of reconciliation, because it is made possible in the first place by the reconciling death of Christ on the cross. This theological discourse lays the basis for Paul to make an anxious appeal to the Corinthians for reconciliation (6:1–13; 7:2–4). Even though Paul does not say so in detail, and even though the theological sections might lead us to believe otherwise, we sense that something is not quite right with Paul's relationship to the Corinthian congregation, and that some unnamed conflict is brewing just below the surface.

At this point in the text, the unsuspecting readers are presented with two contextual difficulties. First of all, the text interjects into the discussion what appears to be a parenthetical remark on misyoking between believers and unbelievers (6:14–7:1). Whatever this passage means, it rudely interrupts Paul's thought in mid-sentence — so much so that the only way to make sense of 6:13 ("In return, open wide your heart... and you... ") is to complete the thought with 7:2 ("... make room for us."). The second difficulty is equally disruptive. The travelogue that begins in 2:12–13 is unceremoniously resumed in 7:5, as if the intervening elaborate discourse on authentic ministry had never been written. The earlier plea on behalf of the wrongdoer in chapter 2 reappears (7:12). But what is truly surprising is that it makes no allusion whatsoever to the theme of reconciliation which he has so laboriously established just a few chapters earlier. One would have thought that the troubles in Corinth were the reason that prompted Paul to launch his theological discussion, and one would expect him to make use of it here. Instead, the text picks up the plea, the travelogue, and Titus's visit as if nothing had taken place in the intervening chapters. Gone are Paul's earlier anxieties over his relationship with the Corinthians; gone are his preoccupations with the unnamed opponents. Instead, Paul beams with optimism and assurance. Towards the end of chapter 7, Paul brightly declares his "complete confidence" in the Corinthians to do the right thing (7:5–16 but especially verse 16).

We can observe the same disjunction between chapters 9 and 10. Chapters 8–9 are in all likelihood a self-contained letter exhorting the Corinthians to contribute to the relief effort for the poor in Jerusalem.[2] In this letter, Paul glows with confidence in the success of the fundraising project, and he is optimistic that the generosity shown here will unite Jewish and gentile churches, thereby bringing glory to God. He is so elated, in fact, and his mood so upbeat that he concludes the letter with a triumphant doxology, "Thanks be to God for his indescribable gift!" (9:15). In the very next sentence, however, all this is gone and we come face to face with an acerbic, ironic, derisive Paul: "It is I myself, Paul, who appeal to you through the meekness and gentleness of Christ — I who am humble in person with you but bold towards you when I am absent" (10:1).

This is just the beginning. He continues accusing the Corinthians of disobedience, even threatening them with discipline during his upcoming visit. He launches his fool's speech with a prolonged catalogue of pains and sufferings. He complains vociferously about the Corinthians' suspicion of his motives and their demand for apostolic credentials. He attacks his opponents, and he attacks them mercilessly. He denounces them as "false apostles," he labels them—with biting sarcasm and more than a little satirical witticism—"super-apostles," he even calls them "Satan's ministers"! On and on he goes. This is obviously a different Paul than the one who has nothing but praise for the Corinthians at the end of chapter 9.

How should we handle all these emotional ups and downs, narrative disruptions, and contextual inconcinnities? The conclusion seems inescapable that our canonical 2 Corinthians is not a continuous composition from start to finish, but is made up of different letters or portions of letters written at different times in Paul's complex, ever-changing, often rancorous relationship with his new converts in Corinth. Given the interruption of Paul's itinerary to Macedonia in 2:12–13 and its resumption in 7:5–16, it seems reasonable to postulate that those two sections belong to the same letter. This means taking the intervening chapters (2:14–7:4) as a separate letter altogether. The only exception is 6:14–7:1, which, judged on the basis of vocabulary and contextual disjunction, is in all probability a non-Pauline insertion, perhaps a marginal gloss that a later copyist inadvertently incorporated into the main text. The same considerations would seem to require that the harsh transition from 9:15 to 10:1 be taken as a literary seam separating two different letters. In that case, chapters 8–9 would belong to a single, self-contained letter of appeal, while chapters 10–13 would be part of a polemical piece composed with the opponents in mind.[3] We can visualize the division and arrangement of the various letters with the help of diagram on the following page.

Events in Corinth: A Reconstruction

We will have to reexamine in greater detail the various contextual dislocations when we discuss the passages in question. For the time being, the reader might use the following reconstruc-

ARRANGEMENT OF LETTERS
INCLUDED IN 2 CORINTHIANS

Letter B 1:1–2:13 & 7:5–16

1:12–14   Paul boasts in the Corinthians and the Corinthians boast in Paul

1:15–22   Paul's original plan to visit the Corinthians on his way to and from Macedonia

1:23–2:4 Paul decided against the visit and wrote a "letter of tears" instead (2:4).

2:5–11   The offender should be forgiven.

2:12–13   Ministry in Troas, but not finding Titus there (at Troas), Paul went to Macedonia.

> *Letter A* 2:14–7:4 (except 6:14–7:1)
>
> 2:14–3:3 Distinction between Paul and other missionaries.
>
> > *Notes: (a) Tone of 1:12–2:13 conciliatory; 2:14–3:3 polemical; (b) Travelogue from Troas to Macedonia dropped until 7:5.*
>
> 3:4–4:6   Ministry of the New Covenant.
>
> 4:7–5:10 Treasure in earthenware vessel.
>
> 5:11–21   Ministry of reconciliation.
>
> 6:1–13   An appeal to the Corinthians.
>
> > 6:14–7:1 Non-Pauline interpolation
>
> 7:2–4   Continuation of appeal that abruptly ends at 7:1.

7:5–16   Titus meets Paul in Macedonia, resuming narrative of 2:12–13.

Notes: (a) The "letter of tears" mentioned again in 7:8 (cf. 2,4); (b) Repentance mentioned again in 7:9–12 (cf. 2:5–11); (c) Tone of 7:5–16 closer to that of 1:12–2:13.

Letter C 8:1–9:15
On the collection for the poor in Jerusalem.

Letter D 10:1–13:10
A severe letter that attacks the opponents and threatens the Corinthians with discipline.

tion of the events behind the Corinthian correspondence as a roadmap to help navigate the tortuous turns found in 2 Corinthians. Paul was the founder of the Corinthian congregation, an event of which Paul never tires of reminding his readers (see, for example, 2 Cor 1:19).[4] After staying there for some eighteen months, according to Acts 18:11–18, Paul was brought before Proconsul Gallio, governor of Achaia and Corinth from 51–52 C.E., ostensibly because local Jewish inhabitants brought a charge against him Some time after that, Paul left the Greek city. Working backward in time, then, we arrive at the dates of early 50 when Paul started his Corinthian mission and the summer of 51 when he departed. Upon his return to Ephesus, his new congregation wrote him at least once for instruction in the new faith. This letter, mentioned in 1 Cor 7:1, is now lost, but it must have prompted Paul, while he was still in Ephesus (1 Cor 16:8), to respond with what has come down to us as the canonical 1 Corinthians. First Corinthians, for its part, is a misnomer, because Paul had written an earlier letter, according to 1 Cor 5:9, to tell his new converts not to become associated with immoral people. But that letter, too, is now lost, and 1 Corinthians remains our earliest surviving letter by the apostle to the city.

Around the same time as the writing of 1 Corinthians or, more likely, soon afterwards, Paul sent Timothy to Corinth as his personal emissary (1 Cor 4:17; 16:10–11), probably for the purpose of coordinating the relief effort for the poor and needy in Jerusalem (1 Cor 16:1–4). But Timothy's mission was evidently unfulfilled; instead, he returned with the disturbing news that a group of itinerant missionaries had made their way to Corinth and had begun to insinuate themselves into the church there.[5] What exactly they did or taught remains a mystery, but Paul clearly perceived them to be a threat. It is equally mysterious as to what kind of threat these newcomers had posed, since Paul responded to them largely in theological terms and then only indirectly. But they might well have been a serious challenge to Paul's status and authority as an apostle. Upon hearing this unsettling news from Titus, Paul composed and sent a letter which included his discourse on the veil of Moses and on the ministry of reconciliation—Letter A which is now partially preserved in 2:14–7:4 (excluding 6:14–7:1)—in the hopes of winning his converts back with a subtle theological argument.

Impetuous as he was, however, Paul evidently did not or could not wait for the Corinthians to respond and decided to make an unexpected visit — his second — to Corinth in an attempt to rescue his apostolate. This move turned out to be disastrous, one to which he would later refer as the "painful visit" (2 Cor 2:1; 7:2). A member of the congregation apparently offended Paul so grievously — perhaps to the point of slandering him publicly according to 2:5-6; 7:12 — that he left Corinth angry and hurt. Home again in Ephesus and feeling disgraced and enraged, Paul wrote what he later called a "letter of tears," to which he refers in 2:4 and again in 7:8. We have little information about the contents of the letter, except that it somehow succeeded in changing the minds of the congregation, so much so that the church was willing to punish the offender as an appeasement to Paul. This time, Titus, not Timothy, brought back to Paul news of this happy event when they met in Macedonia (7:6-7). This would suggest that Titus had been dispatched to Corinth with the letter of tears.

Relieved but anxious to defuse a still-explosive situation, Paul wrote the Corinthians a conciliatory letter that included 1:1–2:13 and 7:5-16 (Letter B). The good news also renewed hope that the original project of collecting contributions for the Jerusalem church could now be completed. In addition to the conciliatory letter, therefore, Paul appended a letter of appeal for funds (Letter C now preserved in its entirety in chapters 8–9). He once again appointed Titus for the trip, no doubt because of his recent success with the congregation (7:13-16). Titus and two unnamed "brothers" would lead an advance delegation to Corinth, in order to put the collection in proper order (8:6, 23) before Paul's arrival (9:4).

The perceived and hoped-for goodwill on all sides turned out to be short-lived, however, for soon we find an exasperated Paul, beleaguered and agitated, defending himself and lashing out at his enemies all at once in an emotion-laden letter (Letter D, partially preserved in chapters 10-13). From Paul's rhetoric, we can be reasonably sure that the Corinthians suspected the delegation headed by Titus of impure motives (12:17-18). To make matters worse, these suspicions were combined with disparaging views on Paul's abilities and apostolic credentials. In response, Paul went on the offensive, attacking the itinerant missionaries once again, but this time openly and directly. He also threatened to discipline the wayward Corinthians once he arrived at Corinth (12:14; 13:2).

Later in his letter to the Romans, which he wrote while he was in Corinth (presumably during his third visit), Paul makes one last mention of the collection effort for Jerusalem—this time he has succeeded in bringing it to a completion (Rom 15:25–26). From this we can infer that the unrest in Corinth must have subsided by the time Paul did make his visit, enough for him to finish collecting the contributions for Jerusalem. We might also postulate that for Paul to compose such a lengthy and nuanced work as Romans, he would have had to make an extended stay in Corinth in relative tranquillity.[6] Nevertheless, if 2 Corinthians 10–13 is indeed Paul's last correspondence with the church, we can also conclude with reasonable certainty that the apostle, bruised and embattled after these ordeals, just turned his attention westward to Spain (Rom 15:24, 28) and left Corinth once and for all.[7]

The probable sequence of events reconstructed on the basis of the Corinthian correspondence can be summarized as follows:

- Founding of the Corinthian church (Acts 18:1–17; 2 Cor 1:19) in early 50 C.E.

- Paul wrote a letter, now lost, advising the Corinthians not to associate with immoral people (1 Cor 5:9).

- The Corinthians sent a letter, now lost, asking for instructions (mentioned in 1 Cor 7:1).

- Paul wrote the canonical 1 Corinthians in response to the questions raised by the congregation.

- Some time later, Paul sent Timothy to Corinth to coordinate the collection effort (1 Cor 4:17; 16:10–11; see 1 Cor 16:1–4).

- Timothy returned with news that itinerant missionaries had visited Corinth.

- Paul wrote a theological discussion of Moses and cosmic reconciliation, partially preserved in 2 Cor 2:14–7:4 (excluding 6:14–7:1)—Letter A—in hopes of winning back the affection of the Corinthians.

- Paul made an unscheduled ("painful") visit to Corinth (2 Cor 2:1; 7:2), during which a member of the Corinthian congregation grievously offended Paul (2 Cor 2:5–6; 7:12), and Paul left Corinth in disgrace.

- Paul wrote the "letter of tears" (2 Cor 2:4; 7:8), now lost, and asked Titus to be the letter-carrier.

- Titus returned to Paul with the good news that the Corinthians had had a change of heart (2 Cor 7:6-7).

- Relieved, Paul wrote a letter of reconciliation (2 Cor 1:1–2:13; 7:5-16) — Letter B — and a letter of appeal for the collection (chaps. 8–9) — Letter C — and dispatched a delegation headed by Titus to Corinth with both letters.

- The Corinthians rejected the appeal, however, and even raised suspicions about Paul's motive behind the collection (2 Cor 12:17-18).

- Exasperated and angry, Paul wrote the ironical "fool's speech" (chaps. 10–13) — Letter D.

- Paul made the "third visit" to Corinth (2 Cor 12:14; 13:1) and completed the collection (Rom 15:25-26).

Can One Read 2 Corinthians Holistically?

Even if one could solve all the literary and historical problems in 2 Corinthians, there remains another hurdle before the readers. After all, the kind of historical and literary problems we have surveyed are relatively familiar to New Testament scholarship, and they have all been discussed thoroughly, even though there may be no consensus on their solutions. But what the modern readers must be vigilant about above all else is the threat that these historical and literary problems will become the be-all and end-all issues that define an "orthodox" method of reading. What stands in the way of a reader's full appreciation of Paul's words in 2 Corinthians is the easy tendency to let the historical and literary problems, however abundantly critical and important they might be, overwhelm all other modes of inquiries and alternative quests for meaning. To conclude that a scenario such as we have proposed above is the ultimate solution to the problem of understanding 2 Corinthians is to say that reading is no more than an exercise in historical reconstruction. To do so is to claim that the letter holds no more significance to the distant readers than the historical information it depicts. To do so is to reduce the text to its context. To do so is to suggest that the text is no more than a mere road sign pointing to something else beyond itself, so that once we reach our final destination we could disregard the sign altogether.

But, in fact, Paul's letter had meaning not just for the historical Corinthian congregation but also for contexts in subsequent generations. That an unknown compiler in the early church took the trouble to stitch the different letters and fragments (if our hypothesis above is correct) into our present 2 Corinthians, and that the letter in turn would be included in a richly diverse canon, are fair indications that some later readers thought what Paul had written in strife had a meaning that could transcend the controversies surrounding the original events. They must have thought that what was constructed in one context, out of one situation, had applications in other contexts and for a wide range of situations. Texts and scriptures can never be isolated from the community of faith; they have become scriptures precisely *because of* the wider community of faith.[8] The challenge for the readers of 2 Corinthians is to reintegrate all the pieces that they have analytically isolated from the texts, to put them back together, to look at the text in the newly invigorated context with renewed fascination, with a kind of "second *naïveté*" of which the philosopher Gabriel Marcel has spoken.[9]

The text therefore holds promise of opening an infinite range of possibilities depending on the new contexts in which it makes its home. What these possibilities are cannot be predetermined or predefined; to do so would make nonsense of the very notion of possibility. Each new generation and each community of readers has to discover, then realize, these possibilities for themselves. All a slender volume such as this can hope to accomplish is to hint at such possibilities. These are ideas, concepts, and actions in 2 Corinthians so singularly important, so fascinating to the readers, so insistent on the fundamental significance of the text that they continue to transcend themselves and lend themselves to meaningful interpretations. In the words of the Catholic theologian David Tracy,

> If, even once, a person has experienced a text, a gesture, an image, an event, a person with the force of the recognition: "This is important! This does make and will demand a difference!" then one has experienced a candidate for classic status. If one's own experience has been verified by other readers, especially by the community of capable readers

over the centuries, the reflective judgment should prove
that much more secure. If the experience is verified at a
later period of life, when a new but related understanding
of the same classic occurs with the same force of revela-
tory power, then, once again, a reflective judgment upon
the realized experience of this text, event, gesture, image,
symbol, person — this structured expression of the human
spirit — is rendered yet more plausible, still more relatively
adequate.[10]

A Context of Controversy:
Rhetoric and Hermeneutics

One of the ways in which we can help detect such pointers
in the text is by means of Paul's rhetoric. Rhetorical analysis
can be, and has often been, little more than a dry academic
exercise, if it places its emphasis solely on Paul's techniques
and formal argumentation. But an examination of rhetorical
devices used in 2 Corinthians can be a way of sensitizing us
to Paul's construction of the problem for his readers and il-
luminates his theological motivation for answering a specific
question. An example will illustrate this relationship between
problem-construction and theological formulation. As we have
seen, Paul is ever-vigilant about the deleterious effects his opponents have had on the Corinthian congregation, but that is
not always how he constructs his problem rhetorically for his
readers. Paul chooses an indirect route to accomplish this. He
opposes these itinerant preachers by appealing to his Corinthian
converts and by reminding them of their relationship to him.
In other words, even though the actual problem comes from
the outside, Paul ignores it and presents it rhetorically as one
between himself and his congregation. Only in chapters 10–13
does Paul address his opponents directly; in the rest of the book,
he chooses instead to remind his hearers of the message of the
cross and its implications: namely, strength through weakness
as exemplified in the death of Christ, as a result of which God
has reconciled the world to God's self in the cosmic drama of
reconciliation. While he is well aware of the outside influences
that constantly undermine his own authority in the community,
he sees in his bond with the new church the key to counter
these centrifugal forces. If he can strengthen this bond, he feels

he could stand up to the outsiders' influence on the Corinthians. Subsequently, it is with this assumption in mind that Paul appeals to the congregation with all the theological acumen available to him. It is a sobering thought that in the history of the Christian church, internecine controversy turns out to be the mother of theology.

While not all the controversies we see in 2 Corinthians are attributable to the outside missionaries, there can be no doubt that they were the principal cause for much of the unrest in the Corinthian church. The unscheduled visit which ended in much pains and tears can well be traced to Paul's distrust of these itinerant preachers. The historical records hold no independent witness to these competitors of Paul's except the latter's obviously biased accounts of them. These missionaries, whom Paul sarcastically calls "super-apostles" (2 Cor 11:5; 12:11), evidently disparaged Paul for being an ineffective speaker (10:10; 11:6), for being devoid of any demonstrable superhuman power (10:10), and for his supposed lack of external credentials like letters of recommendation (cf. 3:1; 5:12). If they did not in fact make these accusations, their strengths in precisely these areas must have prompted the Corinthians to compare Paul unfavorably to them. In other words, they must have boasted of their Jewish pedigree (11:22), their credentials as documented in some letters of recommendation issued by recognized authorities, and their abilities to perform miracles and wonders (12:12). We will discuss their identities more fully in chapter 6 when we examine 2 Corinthians 10–13 in detail. For now it is enough to observe that they greatly resemble a similar group of missionaries who advocated that the Galatians supplement their faith in Christ by taking up circumcision.

Though these charges against Paul might at first appear to be little more than personal attacks, Paul perceived them as an attack on his ministry. Paul after all was the founder of the Corinthian church and his personal character and abilities were intimately related to his apostolic authority, which in the absence of civil or legal structures that might guarantee some sort of power, was the only form of authority available to him in the earliest days of the church. If that was undermined, so would the very foundation of his ministry. An attack on his personal worth was therefore tantamount to questioning the authenticity of his ministry. At the same time, Paul could not identify his ministry too strictly with his personal credentials, as if there were no difference between the two. This was precisely the error of his opponents who amassed their authority on personal prowess and built their ministry as extensions of individual endowments.

In other words, notwithstanding the obvious intensity of the controversy in Corinth, Paul had to navigate carefully between two competing concerns. On the one hand, he must defend his own apostolic authority, without which his ministry would lose its legitimacy. On the other hand, he must make sure that his personal defense did not absolutize his personal credentials, so much so that his ministry might be reduced to a parade of individual abilities. In short, Paul could not engage his opponents by arguing with them directly, for to do so would have ceded to them the grounds and terms of the argument. To match strength for strength with his detractors would have been an endorsement of their operating premise that ministry is to be authenticated by power and strength. If Paul had done that, he might have been able to salvage his personal dignity but would have ultimately lost the debate.

Paul resolved this dilemma by stressing that authentic Christian ministry is in fact not characterized by power and strength but by weakness and suffering, specifically the weakness and suffering of Christ. The Christian story was inaugurated by the paradigmatic sufferings endured by the crucified Jesus, which is a point that Paul has already emphasized in 1 Corinthians. But in 2 Corinthians, he goes beyond his earlier formulation by insisting that his own hardships experienced as a result of proclaiming the gospel — that is to say, his perceived lack of extravagant prowess and elegant presence compared to the super-apostles — is the point at which he identifies with the suffering and death of Christ. As a part of his profound identification with Christ, Paul somehow perceives his personal sufferings and weaknesses to be at the same time Christ's. In this homology between his sufferings and Christ's Paul finds evidence of his union with Christ, a union enriched by mystical and ecstatic encounters but not limited to them. This is the full significance of what earlier scholars have called Paul's "Christ-mysticism."[11] A corollary of such an identification with Christ is that Paul's powerlessness paradoxically demonstrates the energy of God's grace in authentic life and ministry. Just as Christ's humiliation in death unleashes the power of resurrection, so too Paul's weakness brings into sharp relief a ministry of glory. In this regard, the true minister has no cause to boast except that he or she is a faithful conduit for the power of God.

By means of this strategy, then, Paul aims not only at authenticating his apostleship and ministry — thus hopefully retaining his Corinthian converts' devotion to him — but especially at encouraging his readers to follow his example of identification with Christ. What has been experienced by Paul is also available to all believers. Their present possession of the eschatological Spirit guarantees that they, with unveiled faces, can enter into union with Christ directly, without intermediaries. True ministers thus denude their native strengths and empty their own claims. Authentic ministry is at heart kenotic ministry.[12]

Chapter 2

The Civic and Social Context of Second Corinthians

Even as one must interpret 2 Corinthians in the context of first-century intramural controversies between competing missionaries, one inevitably becomes keenly aware of the social and civic matrix from which the Corinthian church emerged. It would be an overstatement to say that this larger context was responsible for the myriad problems in the young church and in their relationship with their founding apostle, just as it would be too simplistic to suggest that Paul's rhetorical and theological formulation in 2 Corinthians could be reduced to controversies standing in the background. Nevertheless, the peculiar cosmopolitanism of the city of Corinth, the character of its society, as well as the general ethos of the first-century Roman Empire that asserted itself in every urban center in the Mediterranean world, could not but contribute to the special character of the Corinthian correspondence as a whole. The dispute over eating food that had been sacrificed to idols, for example, questions about sexual morality, incest, and temple prostitution, the mixture of social classes within the church — all these issues (with which Paul deals in 1 Corinthians mainly) were not unique to the city of Corinth. But the Corinthian context in which they were raised made them that much more urgent in the mind of Paul.

Moreover, issues related to money can only be understood from within the context of Roman social network and relationship. Paul's refusal to accept financial support from the Corinthian congregation, a decision that strained his relationship with them (see 1 Cor 9:8–18; 2 Cor 11:8–9; 12:13), must be seen in light of a patronage system that played an indispensable and determinative role in the social and economic life of Corinthian society.[1] Similarly, the collection project for the poor in the Jerusalem church, on which Paul expended enormous time and energy — not to mention personal prestige — soliciting Greek churches for financial contributions, can only be understood in the context of first-century economic relationship. It behooves us, therefore, to attempt a thicker description of the social and civic life in Corinth before entertaining the biblical text.

The City of Corinth

The first-century city of Corinth which Paul visited and where he founded its first Christian church, in spite of its historical roots going back to Homeric times, was less than a century old. The ancient Greek city upon which Paul's Corinth was rebuilt had been totally devastated in 146 B.C.E. by the Romans for having opposed Rome as a member of the Achaian League. As punishments, its city walls were razed, all buildings burned, its adult males executed, and the rest of the inhabitants captured and sold into slavery.[2] But its favorable location was far too valuable to be ignored for long by its Italian master. In 44 B.C.E., shortly before his assassination, Julius Caesar issued an edict that a new colony be planted on the original site. Before long the city regained its former glory and soon became the leading city of the newly organized province of Achaia and was later chosen as its capital over Athens.[3] Less than half a century after its rebirth, the city was able to win back the right to host the Isthmian games from Sicyon.[4] Towards the end of the first century C.E., the new Corinth was distinguished, among other things, for being one of three banking centers in Greece.[5] Archaeologists have also unearthed evidence of a prosperous period of building projects and public works in the middle of first century C.E.[6]

Wealthy Corinth

Ancient Corinth had always been synonymous with wealth ever since the days of Homer, who referred to the city as "wealthy Corinth" (*Iliad* 2.570), a line also found in Pindar (*Eulogies* 122). Its chief source of income, without a doubt, came from commerce, and what gave Corinth its commercial edge over its rival cities was its superior geography. Sitting astride an isthmus only four miles wide at its narrowest point between the Greek mainland and the Peloponnese, Corinth commanded natural control over all land routes between north and south as no other city in the ancient world. And, having easy access to the Corinthian Gulf to the west via the harbor at Lechaeum — auspiciously situated within its city walls — and the Saronic Gulf to the east through the harbor at Cenchreae, Corinth controlled the sea trades between east and west as well. Instead of braving the weeklong journey through the treacherous waters at the southern tip of the Peloponnese, many sea captains preferred to dock their ships at one of Corinth's two harbors. If their vessels were small enough, they could be lifted out of water, towed across dry land on a paved track (the *diolcos* which joined the Corinthian and Saronic Gulfs), and transported on a wheeled wooden structure (a *holcos*) to the other side. If the vessels were too large for the track, they would be unloaded and their cargoes transferred to ships waiting on the other side. Revenues generated from trades and shipping made Corinth a byword for wealth. To undergird all these commercial activities of the city, financial institutions thrived, making Corinth the banking center that it was. In the words of the geographer Strabo,[7]

> Corinth is called "wealthy" because of its commerce, since it is situated on the Isthmus and is master of two harbours, of which the one leads straight to Asia, and the other to Italy; and it makes easy the exchange of merchandise from both countries that are so far distant from each other. And just as in early times the Strait of Sicily was not easy to navigate, so also the high seas, and particularly the sea beyond Maleae,[8] on account of the contrary winds; and hence the proverb, "But when you double Maleae forget your home." At any rate, to land their cargoes here was a welcome alternative to the voyage to Maleae for merchants from both Italy and Asia. And also the duties on what was exported by land from the Peloponnese as well as on what was imported into it belonged to those who held the keys. And to later times this remained ever so. But to the Corinthians of later times still greater advantages were added, for also the Isthmian games, which were celebrated there, were wont to draw crowds of people (*Geography* 8.6.20a).[9]

Another source of income for Corinthians was the Isthmian games, which Strabo mentioned in the quote above. These games were one of four panhellenic festivals, ranking just below the games held at Olympia but above those at Delphi and Nemea.[10] Staged every two years, the Isthmian games were vital not only to the prestige of the city but especially to its wealth. The games were enormously costly to sponsor, as the following inscription, dedicated to the first sponsor of the newly revived Isthmian games, attests:

> [To Lucius Castricius Regulus..., agonothete of the Isthmian and the Caesarean games, who was [the first] to preside over the Isthmian games at the Isthmus under the sponsorship of Colonia Laus Julia Corinthiensis. He introduced [poetry contests in honor of] the divine Julia Augusta, and [a contest for] girls, and after *all the buildings of Caesarea were renovated,* he... completed [*the construction of a stoa* (?)], and *gave a banquet for all the inhabitants* of the colony.[11]

This inscription tells us that it was the responsibility of the president to bear all the costs of the games, which must have been immense. These included renovating all the buildings *and* bearing the cost of a banquet for everyone in the city. One could not but be astounded by the enormous wealth one single individual could amass less than fifty years after the founding of the colony. In spite of the high cost for hosting the games, the festivities and pageantry were sure to attract a large number of visitors and participants. Needless to say, all this provided a steady stream of income to the city treasury.

A third source of income to the city was, perhaps not surprisingly for a busy seaport such as Corinth, the prevalence of temple prostitution. As famous as Corinth was for its wealth, it was even better known for debauchery. Aristophanes, the Athenian comic poet (450–385 B.C.E.), coined the verb *Korinthiazesthai* meaning "to act like a Corinthian," that is, "to fornicate."[12] Strabo had reported that the temple of Aphrodite in Acrocorinth had housed more than one thousand prostitutes (*Geography* 8.6.20c). From available literary and archaeological evidence, however, one might question the accuracy of Strabo's account. The context in which the account is set suggests that he was describing the temple in ancient Corinth, though it is unclear what his source was. In his own visit of Roman Corinth in 29 B.C.E. he reported having seen only a "small temple of Aphrodite" on the summit (*Geography* 8.6.21b), a description corroborated two hundred years later by Pausanias when he

visited the same site (*Description of Greece* 5.1). Recent archaeological evidence also indicates that no such building as capable
of housing that many prostitutes could be found associated with
the temple. Nevertheless, there must be some truth in the continuation of such a reputation, even if accounts of pre-146 B.C.E.
Corinth were somewhat exaggerated. Reports of such activities
found in similar seaports around the empire would suggest that
Corinth was no worse than the rest. One could reasonably postulate that income from these visits continued to fuel the economy
of the new colony.

A further source of income to the city can be attributed to
manufacturing, though this is less than certain. The city had
been famous in classical times for crafting highly sought-after
Corinthian bronze. This reputation continued in the first century, as Plutarch and Pliny have attested, Strabo corroborates
this general reputation of the city:

> The city of Corinth, then, was always great and wealthy,
> and it was well equipped with men skilled in both in
> the affairs of state and in the craftsman's arts; for both
> here and in Sicyon the arts of painting and modeling and
> all such arts of the craftsman flourished most (*Geography*
> 8.6.23d).[13]

But it remains questionable whether we can trust Strabo's report
here. When he visited the city in 29 B.C.E., it had been colonized for barely fifteen years. While the commercial base could
be expected to thrive in so short a time because of Corinth's
advantageous geography, the manufacturing and marketing of
crafts aboard would conceivably take much longer to reestab-
lish. A bronze foundry has been unearthed in Roman Corinth,
but it seems that at this time it was producing crafts intended
only for local use and not for export.[14] In fact, we have archaeological evidence that a good deal of Roman pottery and wares
were imported to Corinth rather than the other way around.[15]
Furthermore, according to Strabo again, the Corinthian terra-
cotta vessels and bronze were so highly prized that many took
to grave-robbing at the time of colonial settlement to satisfy the
demands for them.[16] This is further indication that the manufacturing base had not actually been revived by the first century
C.E. Evidence would suggest that other cities by the first century
were making imitation "Corinthian" wares, especially Corinthian bronze. The industry was started, no doubt, during the

century of Corinth's absence in the Mediterranean market.[17] In the last analysis, it is best to take Strabo's statement here, like many of his other ones in *Geography,* as a generalization based on the venerable reputation which Corinth had enjoyed in the past, not on the actual state of affairs in the early days of Roman Corinth.

Social Mobility and Status Inconsistency

As a result of the short history of the colony and the general Roman pattern of colonization, few among the population in Roman Corinth, at least compared to other cities of greater antiquity, came from the old patrician class. When Corinth was reestablished, Julius Caesar might have colonized it with veterans, according to late first-century report by Plutarch.[18] But if that was indeed the case, veterans constituted at best only a minority. It is far more likely that mostly former slaves and citizens from the lower classes were sent to the new colony.[19] Crinagoras (b. 70 B.C.E.), possibly an eyewitness to the Roman proceedings when plans were being drawn up for the repopulation of Corinth, lamented this turn of misfortune for the once proud ancient city:

> What inhabitants, O luckless city, have you received, and in place of whom? Alas for the general calamity to Greece! Would, Corinth, that you be lower than the ground and more desert than the Libyan sands, than wholly abandoned to such a *crowd of scoundrelly slaves,* you should vex the bones of the ancient Bacchiadae" (*Anthology* 9.284).[20]

Strabo confirmed that the Roman colonizers sent to Corinth were mostly former slaves (*Geography* 8.6.23c), while the historian Appian (95–c. 165) related that it was "the poor" who had asked Julius Caesar for land and had been granted permission to go to Carthage and Corinth (*History* 8.136). It is not immediately clear what "poor" means exactly, but it may be best to see them as "those who felt themselves locked into a certain social level through lack of opportunity."[21]

A result of such a mixed demography is relative mobility between the social classes in Corinth. The distinguished citizens in Corinth were of the merchant class who had no inherited status but plenty of opportunities to amass enormous wealth. It was easy to become wealthy by trade, even if one had little or no social standing by Roman standards. Furthermore, the merchant class had a great deal of mobility, since travel and trade went hand in hand. What was true for merchants in the empire in general was doubly true for those of Corinth, who could reach Asia and Italy with ease.[22] With extensive travel came the acquisition of knowledge, cross-pollination of ideas, and free exchange of philosophical and religious ideas. All this contributed to a deep yearning for moving beyond one's social class acquired from birth. Yet, because of the rigid class structure in Roman society, one was prevented from fulfilling these expectations, no matter how much wealth one succeeded in accumulating.

Wealth and status often go hand in hand, but, when they do not, tension appears. This is tension between what one expects to become by one's achievements and what society denies a person because of predefined boundaries — whether these boundaries are understood in terms of class, gender, race or ethnicity, or social class. The tension is between what might be called *achieved status* — that is, status gained as a result of accomplishment — and *attributed status* — that is, what one is born with, the given status in life based on breeding, race, or inherited station in life. Sociologists have dubbed this phenomenon of conflicting expectations high *status inconsistency* and low *status crystallization.*[23] One could easily see how this problem was most acute among the noveaux riches of the merchant class in Roman Corinth, for whom the status earned through accomplishment was much higher than the status determined by birth. The restlessness spawned by such status inconsistency tilled the soils in which Paul's message of faith-based egalitarianism took root.

Converts of the Church in Corinth

The social patterns in the general population appear to be reflected in the Corinthian church as well. There is no evidence that any of the church members belonged to the senatorial or equestrian classes. Paul draws upon this fact to mock the Corinthians' factiousness and pretentious claims to the grandiose: "Consider your own call, brothers and sisters: not many of you were *wise* by human standards, not many were *powerful,* not many were of *noble birth.* But God chose what is foolish in the world to shame the wise; God chose what is weak in the world to shame the strong; God chose what is low and despised in the world, things that are not, to reduce to nothing things that are, so that no one might boast in the presence of God" (1 Cor 1:26–29). By the same token, however, no one seems to have come from the bottom of society either: that is, the unskilled laborers, the destitute, the beggars, the peasants.[24] The Corinthian congregation appears to draw its members from freedmen and freedwomen, slaves, merchants, and artisans. A number of these were house-owners, patriarchs with households, people with the means of supporting itinerant missionaries and sponsoring assemblies in their houses.

This general picture could be made more concrete by studying the Corinthians named in Paul's letters. Many of these were drawn from the ranks of well-to-do urbanites, though few of them would be of the aristocratic class. Three names in 1 Corinthians are particularly helpful in giving us concrete information about the congregation's social standings in society: Crispus, Gaius, and Stephanas, all mentioned in 1 Cor 1:14, 16 as having been baptized by Paul. Stephanas and his household, in addition, are identified as the "first converts" in Greece (1 Cor 16:15). Judged by the tendency of the Corinthians to divide their loyalty according to their baptizers and Paul's statement that he did not baptize any of the other Corinthians (1 Cor 1:11–17) — that is, *after* the church had been founded — Crispus and Gaius must have been among Paul's first converts as well.[25]

According to Acts 18:8, Crispus was an *archisynagogos* (i.e., a leader of a local synagogue). If this is the same person mentioned in 1 Cor 1:14, which many scholars take to be the case, then one could be sure that he was a person of high leadership quality and one with financial means. It is unclear whether Jews had high social standings in Roman Corinth; Acts 18, which recounts the failure of Jewish leaders to bring charges against Paul, appears to suggest that the Jews had little influence in the civic government of Corinth. If the Acts account can be trusted, Crispus might not have had a high profile in circles outside the synagogue and the church. Still, it is a reasonable guess that Crispus commanded high respect within the church and might have been one of its leaders.

According to Rom 16:23, Gaius hosted Paul, presumably for an extended period of time so as to provide Paul the necessary resource and time to compose his elaborate letter to the Romans. His wealth, we can surmise, must have been impressive. This is confirmed by the report that his house was large enough to

allow the congregation to have its meetings. Like Crispus, therefore, Gaius was most likely a leader of the church and a man of
means, but does not seem to have been an outstanding citizen in
Corinthian society at large.

Stephanas in 1 Cor 16:15 is identified as the head of a household and he is mentioned in the same passage with Fortunatus
and Achaicus (verse 17). The last two were common names
for slaves in the first century, and were most likely slaves of
Stephanas.[26] Though nothing in Roman society would prevent
them from becoming wealthy, these two probably come from
humble backgrounds. Stephanas, therefore, like Gaius, was a patriarch and a man of independent means. Paul's commendation
for Stephanas and his slaves in 1 Cor 16:15–18 seems somewhat
out of place, since the context does not call for it. It may well
be that Stephanas did not command the same respect by the
Corinthians as either Gaius or Crispus, even though all three
had been baptized by Paul, which is probably an indication that
Stephanas did not have as much social prominence and wealth
as the others named.[27] This would account for Paul's emphasis
on the need to pay them the due respect.

Other prominent members of the Corinthian congregation
are also mentioned in Paul's correspondence. Prisca and Aquila
(1 Cor 16:19), friends of Paul in Corinth who are also mentioned in Acts 18:2 (as Aquila and *Priscilla*), are identified as
heads of a house church in Rom 16:5 (see also Acts 19:22). Their
house-ownership and ability to travel from city to city would
suggest that they also belonged to the merchant class. One could
draw the same conclusion about the economic and social classes
to which Chloe belonged. "Chloe's people" are mentioned in
1 Cor 1:11 as having reported to Paul about the contentiousness
in Corinth when he was in Ephesus. Probably the best way to
understand the phrase is that it refers to Chloe's slaves, freedpersons, or her clients.[28] Their ability to travel to bring news
to Paul in Ephesus, again, points to Chloe's economic status as
belonging to the merchant class. Chloe must have been a powerful leader and deeply involved in the internal struggles of the
Corinthian church.[29]

Erastus, another name connected with the congregation in
Corinth, is identified as a "treasurer (Greek, *oikonomos*) of the
city" in Rom 16:23. He may well be the aedile ("business man-
ager for city"), the overseer of public works, named in an
inscription unearthed near the theater of Roman Corinth: "Eras-

tus in return for his aedileship laid (the pavement) at his own expense."[30] If this is indeed the same person as the Erastus of Rom 16:23, he would be one of a few persons in the Corinthian congregation who had high social standing outside the church. He would be someone with wealth and would be a significant benefactor in the church.[31] It is possible that Erastus was a public slave,[32] but even public slaves in the first century could still accumulate enormous wealth and enjoy social mobility.[33] All this would confirm the judgment of Wayne Meeks regarding the social makeup of the Corinthian church:[34]

> It is hardly surprising that we meet no landed aristocrats, no senators, *equites* [i.e., equestrians], nor (unless Erastus might qualify) decurions [i.e., local senators]. But there is also no specific evidence of people who are of the poor, peasants, agricultural slaves, and hired agricultural day laborers.... The "typical" Christian... is a free artisan or small trader.... Some of the wealthy provided housing, meeting places, and other services for individual Christians and for whole groups. In effect, they filled the roles of patrons.

Roman Patronage
and the Corinthian Church

Phoebe, for whom Romans 16 is a letter of recommendation, is called a *diakonos* and a *prostatis* to Paul and others (Rom 16:2). The title of *diakonos* (literally, "deacon") would make her a leader in the Corinthian church. When this is seen in connection with her ability to travel from city to city, it would lead us to the same conclusion as reached before concerning the likes of Chloe, Prisca, and Aquila. She was in all likelihood a woman of wealth and belonged to the same group of merchants who had the means and needs to travel within the empire.[35] In this regard, she could also be a patron to the church. This role of hers may in fact be indicated by her other title, *prostatis,* which might well mean a "patroness."[36] If this is indeed the case, this would be direct evidence that the Roman patronage system existed as an integral part of the Corinthian church, thus corroborating Meeks's general observation in the quote above. Accordingly, we can now better appreciate the possibility that someone like Gaius might well have been a patron to Paul, furnishing him with the necessary means to continue his ministry over an extended period of time. To understand the context in which 2 Corinthians was written, therefore, it seems indispensable also to understand also how the patron-client relationship affected life in Roman Corinth in general and, in particular, how it might have played a vital role in the Corinthian church.

To gauge the importance of the patronage system in Co-rinthian society, it may be helpful to revisit the inscription dedicated to Lucius Castricius Regulus, the first patron of the Isthmian games in Roman Corinth. The cost of hosting the game, as we have seen, was prohibitively high: it included sponsor-ing the games and providing food and drink for all citizens, and all the expenses were borne by the president himself. The games were obviously vital to the economic health of the city: all facets of civic life were affected by them, and all citizens — from artisans to shop owners — would benefit economically from the large number of visitors pouring into the city for the fes-tivities. In sponsoring the games, the president directly passed material benefits to the citizens, while he himself would gain public recognition (literally etched in stone), prestige, wealth, and power. In so doing, the president became the patron of the city, and the citizens became his clients. This is illustrative of the importance of the patronage system to the social and economic life in Corinth.

The patronage system played an integral role not only in Roman Corinth, but evidently also — if our survey of named members of the Corinthian church is indicative — in Paul's con-gregation. Paul's attitude towards the patronage system seems ambiguous at best. At times, he clearly benefits from his patron-client relationship with the wealthy house-owner Gaius, who provided him the necessary means personally, so that he could continue his ministry. At other times, however, he is also known to have rejected financial support from the Corinthians (1 Cor 9:8-18), while accepting money from the Macedonians (2 Cor 11:8-9; 12:13).[37] What accounts for this inconsistency? More important, why would Paul's refusal to accept money from the Corinthians cause so much controversy?

According to a summary by John Chow, research conducted in the last forty years on the Roman patronage system has yielded the following common features:[38]

- A patron-client relation is an exchange relationship: that is, both sides benefit from the relationship, albeit in different ways.

- A patron-client relation is an asymmetrical relation — in that the patron is a power-broker to whom his or her clients must pay obeisance.

- As a result, a patron-client relation is a hierarchical or vertical relation: it binds the patron and clients together but discourages horizontal relations between clients.

- An implication of the verticality of the relationship is that a patron-client relation benefits only those involved in that particular relation. Benefits cannot be universalized to those outside that relation. A patron-client relation therefore observes strict boundaries that separate one relation from another.

- A patron-client relation is a supralegal relation that is not guaranteed by any legal system but is based on mutual understanding.

- A patron-client relationship is often binding and long-term, because it is based on personal obligations from one party to the other.

- Because a patron-client relation is not based on law but on interpersonal relation, it is a voluntary relation. By the same token, however, a unilateral dissolution of a patron-client relation can lead to ill-feelings and, worse, open hostility or animosity.

It should be pointed out that the roles of patron and client are not mutually exclusive, as if one could only be a patron or a client at any one time, but not both. A freedman, for example, would have his former master as patron above him, but he himself might own slaves he might free one day who would become his clients. Everyone, therefore, can potentially be involved in a complex of vertical relations.

What was true with Corinthian society in general was equally true with the Corinthian church. Paul's refusal to accept money from the Corinthians — which is tantamount to refusing to accept the patronage of the Corinthian congregation — would have to be explained in this light. According to a recent study, itinerant preachers in the first century could support themselves in four ways: by begging, by charging a fee, by working, and by coming under the patronage of a household.[39] Paul elected to work for a living in order to support his ministry; according to accounts in Acts, he worked as a tentmaker. But if Paul was working well within the boundaries of commonly accepted social practices of his days, why should that be controversial within the Corinthian community?

We can answer this question by examining how Paul defends himself. In 1 Corinthians 9, before Paul answers the question why he has refused money from the Corinthian church, Paul poses a series of rhetorical questions: "Am I not free? Am I not an apostle? Have I not seen our Lord Jesus Christ? Are you yourselves not my work in the Lord? If I am not an apostle to others, I am indeed one to you. For you yourselves are my seal of the letter in the Lord" (1 Cor 9:1–2). The strengthening of apostolic qualification by means of reiterating his vision of the resurrected Lord ("Have I not seen our Lord Jesus Christ?") was a common strategy, since it was understood that apostleship was legitimated by such a vision. Later Paul makes direct reference to this connection between vision and legitimation in 1 Cor 15:1–11. But Paul's concern to buttress his apostolic claim in 1 Corinthians 9 would indicate that his refusal to accept financial support and patronage from the Corinthians had something to do with the legitimacy of his apostleship.

We are now closer to understanding why Paul's action was so controversial to the Corinthians: If the question of his apostleship stands in the background of this controversy, there must have been *some other apostles* who *did accept* Corinthian support, as a result of which Paul was cast in negative light. In other words, while Paul elected to work for a living and to become independent of the Corinthian patronage, there were other itinerant preachers who happily accepted money from the church. This may in fact be indicated in 1 Cor 9:6: "Do we not have the right to our food and drink? Do we not have the right to be accompanied by a wife, as do the other apostles and the brothers of the Lord and Cephas? Or is it only Barnabas and I who have no right to refrain from working for a living?" Paul argues that he, too, has the same rights as all other apostles, rights which would include being paid by the community. It is not a gift from a wealthy patron but something he could claim because of his position as an apostle. He continues in 9:12: "If *others* share this rightful claim on you, do not we still more?" We will not need to concern ourselves with the identity of "other," since these may well constitute a different group of opponents than those with whom Paul has to contend in 2 Corinthians. It is enough for our purpose to show that there are those who do accept payment from the church for their service. The Corinthians would prefer that Paul come under the same arrangement, but Paul insists that it is his right, which means that he could claim it or—as he chooses to do—to refuse it.

This, of course, only pushes the question one step further, since it explains why the Corinthians were unhappy with Paul's refusal to accept patronage, but it does not explain why Paul himself refused to accept it in the first place. What complicates this question is that Paul did not always refuse money. In 2 Cor 11:8–9, he does acknowledge that he accepts money from churches in Macedonia: that is, churches in Thessalonica and Philippi. Moreover, Paul was not above living under the patronage of Gaius. If we are to judge the complexity of his letter to the Romans, which he wrote while he was in Corinth, the patronage of Gaius must have lasted a long time. At bottom, it is the inconsistency of Paul's actions that must have caused a great deal of the controversy referred to in 2 Corinthians. To complicate the situation even more: Paul was also making a serious effort at completing the collection project for the poor in the Jerusalem church. His rejection of money on the one hand and active pursuit of it on the other, when seen against the background of Roman patronage, could not but confuse the Corinthians and raise suspicion about his character.

All this seems to raise the possibility that Paul would accept money only *on his own terms.* He emphasizes in 1 Corinthians 9 that every worker deserves his or her wages, and as an apostle he, too, would deserve a fair wage. To be receiving financial support from the church *under the patronage system,* however, would have made Paul a client which would, in turn, compromise his independence and, more importantly, his apostolic position in the hierarchy. He accepted money, then, presumably when he could do so on his own terms, when his own apostolic authority could be preserved. In short, Paul's refusal to take money for his service was part and parcel of his attempt at renegotiating with an underlying assumption that power and authority were based on the Roman patronage system.[40] This will become clearer when we examine the relevant passages in the text, to which our next chapter turns.

Chapter 3

A Letter of Reconciliation: 1:1-2:13 and 7:5-16

First-time readers of 2 Corinthians might be lured into an easy sense of familiarity if they happen to have studied Paul's other letters. We find all the major epistolary elements we have come to expect from a letter by Paul, elements such as the opening salutation, thanksgiving, travelogue, even the closing benediction and greetings. Paul adapted first-century letter-writing techniques from the Greco-Roman world to early Christian missionary circles so successfully that these formal components have become permanent fixtures in all his letters, and we notice them only when they are absent. Take, for instance, the extreme case of Galatians, which might seem quite conventional at first but soon catches the unsuspecting reader by surprise. The salutation of Gal 1:1-5 is rather standard. It is wordier than most, but is not the longest among Paul's surviving letters (Rom 1:1-7 is). It contains a threefold delineation of apostleship ("not from human beings, nor through human beings, but through Jesus Christ and God the Father who raised him from the dead," verse 1), but is otherwise unremarkable. By the time we come to verse 6, however, instead of finding his customary thanksgiving prayer (for example, 1 Thess 1:2, "We thank God always for all of you"), we are jolted by the blunt "I am amazed that you are turning so quickly away from the one who called you in grace into another gospel!" At this juncture in the text we — and no doubt his intended Galatian readers as well — are only too aware that we are about to come under attack from Paul's seething prose. Sure enough, the rest of Galatians unfolds a barrage of verbal assaults on the Galatians. Paul chides them for being willingly seduced by outside agitators (1:6-9); he calls them "foolish Galatians!" (3:1); he scolds them for believing in the gospel in vain (4:11); he mocks his opponents for advocating circumcision (5:11).

Not so with 2 Corinthians. In spite of the developing troubles in the Corinthian church with internal dissent and with the so-called "false apostles" which we surveyed in chapter 1, we detect no violation of epistolary form and we are subjected to no literary cudgel. Everything seems to be in its rightful place. The thoroughly conventional salutation (2 Cor 1:1) is followed by an equally ordinary greeting (verse 2), and then the prayer of thanksgiving ensues (verses 3–11) — except, however, when we examine the prayer closely, it is not a thanksgiving at all but a *blessing* to God. Whenever Paul writes a thanksgiving prayer, he invariably begins with "I thank God" or some such variation (see Rom 1:8; 1 Cor 1:4; Phil 1:3; 1 Thess 1:2; Philem 4). The only departures from this well-honed pattern are Galatians and our 2 Corinthians. If we learn anything from Galatians, it is that this is no accident.

One obvious answer is that Paul is not as angry at the Corinthians as he is at the Galatians — not yet, in any case, but chapters 10–13 will tell us otherwise. Yet he feels sufficiently uneasy about his relationship with the congregation that he deviates from his normal routine. In so doing, Paul communicates enough of his displeasure that he draws his readers' attention to it, but not so much as to castigate them with heavy reproach before he absolutely has to. His readers in Corinth, in spite of unspoken misgivings, are also likely to appreciate this subtler approach. From 2:5–11 we see that the Corinthians have made a concerted effort at gesturing toward a compromise, if not outright reconciliation, by disciplining one of their own members who had grievously offended Paul.

But it is possible that Paul has a deeper purpose in mind when he uses a blessing instead of a thanksgiving to introduce the body of the letter. It may have to do with establishing an argumentative strategy, to be pursued not in terms of his stormy relationship with the Corinthians, even though that is precisely what is in the forefront of his readers' mind, but in terms of what God has done for him, for the Corinthians, and most importantly for their common experience together. A thanksgiving prayer, at least insofar as it has been transformed by Paul's rhetorical practice, always highlights the recipients' faith and witness (see, e.g., Rom 1:8; 1 Cor 1:4; Phil 1:3–5; 1 Thess 1:3, 7–8; Philem 4–7). But a blessing by its very nature stresses the centrality of God and God's attributes and actions. Whereas a thanksgiving prayer puts the focus on human accomplishments — inasmuch as unwavering faith, steadfast love, and witness of the gospel could be called accomplishments — a blessing draws attention to what God has done: God consoles the afflicted and rescues the despairing. It is these actions of God that create the common bond between the writer and readers, between Paul and the Corinthians, and it is these same actions that should form the common basis for life in the future.[1] In using a blessing as opening, therefore, Paul eschews launching a direct assault at the intransigence of his readers or trying to match wits with his opponents. Instead, Paul hopes to outflank the latter by reminding the Corinthians of their experiences together in affliction and in consolation. All these take place under the aegis of God's supervision and for the sake of a ministry that is to be shared equally by Paul and the Corinthians.

Salutation and Blessing:
1:1–11

1 [1]Paul, an apostle of Christ Jesus through the will of God, and Timothy my brother, to the church of God that is in Corinth with all the saints in the whole of Achaia. [2]Grace to you and peace from God our Father and the Lord Jesus Christ.

[3]Blessed is God and Father of our Lord Jesus Christ, the father of mercies and God of every consolation, [4]who consoles us in our every affliction, so that we may be able to console those in every affliction through the consolation with which we ourselves are consoled by God. [5]Because just as the sufferings of Christ overflow into us, through Christ our consolation also increases. [6]If we are afflicted, it is for the sake of your consolation and salvation; if we are consoled, it is for the aim of your consolation becoming effective as you endure the same sufferings we ourselves also suffer. [7]And our hope is strengthened for you, because we know that as you share in our sufferings, you also share in our consolation.

[8]For we do not wish you to be unaware, brothers and sisters, of our affliction in Asia, that we were burdened to an extraordinary degree, beyond our ability, so that we despaired even of living. [9]But we felt that we had received the death sentence, that we might not count on ourselves but on God who

raises the dead — [10]who has saved us from so deadly a peril and will save us, on whom we have hope that he will also continue to save us — [11]as you also join in helping us by prayer, so that many may render thanks on our behalf for the gift of grace to us which comes as a result of the prayers of many.

The salutation, 1:1–2, as mentioned earlier, is conventionally Pauline. He identifies himself as "an *apostle* of Christ Jesus through the will of God," an important title he often feels denied him. This perceived slight profoundly affects his relationship to other churches as well. In Galatians, for example, where he suspects outsiders threaten his authority, he is at pains to dispel any doubts about the divine origins of his apostolic appointment. And he does so right from the beginning, introducing himself as "an apostle — not from human beings nor through human agency but through Jesus Christ and God the Father who raised him from the dead" (Gal 1:1). He then goes to great length assuring his readers that immediately after his call he "consulted no flesh and blood." In other words, he insists on independence from the Jerusalem church by showing that he never journeyed there until much later and that he went to Arabia instead before returning to Damascus (Gal 1:16–24).

Paul's self-designation in 2 Corinthians, by comparison, is less strident and less insistently defensive, but the perceived threat to his apostleship is no less real. We can fill in the picture of Paul's struggle with the Corinthian congregation over the question of apostleship with information gathered from 1 Corinthians, which incidentally begins with an almost identical salutation ("Paul, called to be an apostle of Christ Jesus through the will of God," 1 Cor 1:1). There appear to be two main causes for the Corinthians' skepticism of Paul: one has to do with money, the other has to do with the source of Paul's authority.

It emerges that the Corinthians, a relatively well-to-do congregation, have been more than a little upset at Paul's refusal to accept financial assistance from them (1 Cor 9:12). Financial assistance, as we have seen in chapter 2, formed the backbone of the patron-client relationship in first-century Roman society and probably played an indispensable role in the support of itinerant missionaries traveling from city to city. When Paul refuses to accept any money from the Corinthian congregation, it may well have been his wish to maintain his independence (see, for example, 1 Cor 9:15–18). But the congregation naturally interprets this action as contrary to the patronage system, an obstacle to the ongoing missionary efforts, and therefore a diminution of his apostolic authority.[2] As we will see in the following chapters, this problem continues to haunt Paul also in 2 Corinthians, even as he redoubles his effort at completing a collection for the church in Jerusalem.

To his critics, Paul replies bitterly, "Am I not free? Am I not an apostle? Have I not seen Jesus our Lord? Are you yourselves not my work in the Lord? If to others I am not an apostle, to you I am, for you yourselves are the seal stamped on my apostleship" (1 Cor 9:1–2). What is remarkable about this apologia is that not only does he remind the Corinthians that they are indebted to him — after all they are *his* converts and therefore his freedom from any constraint should be a foregone conclusion. In addition, he also finds it necessary to emphasize his experience of having seen the resurrected Lord, "Have I not seen Jesus our Lord?" Paul is keenly aware that vision of Christ is what legitimates his authority and authenticates his apostleship. Unlike the "acknowledged pillars" of the church, Peter, John, and James, Paul always feels as if he is at a disadvantage for not having direct, personal knowledge of the earthly Jesus. Nevertheless, Paul makes up for it by stressing the resurrection appearances that he shares with these same unquestioned authorities. Just as Peter, the Twelve, the five hundred brothers and sisters, James, and all the apostles have seen the Lord in his glory (1 Cor 15:5–7), so finally he, Paul, as one "untimely born," was also granted the vision that made him "the least of the apostles" (verse 9a). He adds a further proof of his apostleship: Since he has no intrinsic right to be an apostle because of his former persecution of the church (verse 9b), that he became such a one must have been the result of sheer grace, an unqualified divine appointment by God (verse 10; see also Gal 1:13, 23).[3]

With the blessing of 1:3–11, we begin to move into the main thoughts of 2 Corinthians. Scholars have long noted that Paul's thanksgiving prayers normally function to forecast and anticipate major themes to be elaborated and pursued in the main body of the letter.[4] Even though in 2 Corinthians Paul replaces the thanksgiving with a blessing (for reasons of recasting his structure of argumentation as we discussed earlier), he uses it to maintain his customary practice of announcing main lines to his argument. Paul introduces two correlative themes here: affliction and consolation. While both touch upon deep structures of Paul's theology, they also play an integral part in his argumentative strategy. "Consolation" and its verb "to console" appear a total of ten times in verses 3–7; in addition, the related term "rescue" appears three more times in verses 8–11 (all three occurrences are found in verse 10), "salvation" once (verse 6), and "mercies" once (verse 3). "Affliction," on the other hand, and its verb "to be afflicted" appear four times (verses 4 twice, 6, 8); the related terms "suffer" and "suffering" appear no fewer than four times (verses 5, 6 twice, 7). This high concentration of suffering- and consolation-words in these nine verses thus anticipates the so-called "catalogues of hardships" of 4:8–9; 6:4–5; 11:23b–27, which in the early church were marks of authentic apostles.

This, however, is not to say that Paul invented his experiences just to score points with his interlocutors. There is no reason to doubt that the troubles he encountered in Asia, nearly losing his life (verse 8), reflect the real perils a first-century Christian missionary like Paul must have encountered. Asia was a Roman senatorial province in modern-day Turkey, whose capital, the coastal city of Ephesus, was the major key city of trade and commerce. According to Acts this is where Paul had spent three years and from where Paul made several missionary trips to Macedonia (Philippi, 16:11–40; Thessalonica, 17:1–9) and to Corinth. It is also in Ephesus where Paul was jailed; while in prison Paul sent his letters to Philemon (Philm 10) and to the Philippians (Phil 1:17). According to Phil 1:19–24, Paul also appears to be under threat of life. Whether this near-death experience is behind his cryptic description of 1:8–9 or the equally cryptic statement, "I fought with wild animals at Ephesus" (1 Cor 15:32), we cannot be certain.

Affliction so presented goes to the heart of Paul's theology, and this is something Paul will draw on heavily to develop an argumentative strategy against his opponents and anyone who ventures to drive a wedge between him and his congregation. His plan is to appeal to the sufferings of Christ which form the common experience binding Paul and his Corinthian converts together. Just as he appeals to the crucified Christ defeating worldly wisdom and temporal power with his death and weakness (1 Cor 1:17; 2:1–5), so too here in 2 Cor 1:3–7 he reiterates the same theme of power through weakness, but with a personal and polemical twist. Responding to the boasting of his opponents, who by their demonstration of oratory skills and miraculous powers seduce the Corinthians away from himself, Paul could meet this challenge in one of two ways. Either he tries to match the false apostles' mighty claims, in which case even if he were to win the argument he in effect would have to concede that authentic ministry goes hand in hand with a ostentatious display of strength and might. He would thus cede the terms of the debate to his opponents. Or, Paul could try to change the terms of the debate altogether by arguing for a different basis for boasting, namely, to demonstrate one's power through weakness. This is precisely what Paul has done in the opening blessing. While his opponents bask in the glory of their achievements, Paul places the emphasis squarely on his weakness, his afflictions, and his sufferings — all for the sake of the ministry. These are not absolute goods in themselves; Paul gives no indication of the Jewish idea of righteous suffering as an acceptable offering to God.[5] Rather, Paul emphasizes that his own frailty brings into sharp relief the saving power of God, so that the weaker Paul is, the greater measure is God's grace working upon Paul in rescuing and consoling him in the midst of his hardship (verses 3–4). From this one can easily draw the reverse implication: The more power the human agent displays, the less the grace of God can be documented. By paying such an inordinate amount of attention to affliction and divine consolation, then, Paul turns his critics' strengths into a disadvantage for them, while turning their criticisms of him into an advantage for himself.

What gives Paul purchase on the paradoxical notion of power through weakness is neither megalomania nor self-delusion but an identification with the sufferings of Christ that is, for lack of a better term, mystical. It is not immediately evident what Paul means by the expression "sufferings of Christ" (verse 5), but since Christ's sufferings "overflow into" him, it must have the same reference as "our every affliction, . . . in every affliction" of verse 4, "the same sufferings we ourselves also suffer" of verse 6, and "our sufferings" of verse 7. If that is the case, Paul suggests here that in some sense his sufferings are to be identified with Christ's. The phrase "sufferings of Christ" is used only one other time in Paul's writings, in Phil 3:10, where Paul makes this identification explicit: His aim is "to know him and the power of his resurrection and the sharing of his sufferings, being transformed into his death."[6] In other words, he interprets his personal afflictions in some sense as Christ's sufferings, and that is part and parcel of his conforming to the image of Christ. This is not an emulation of Christ but for Paul an identification — a mystical union — that understands Christ's sufferings as taking place in the life of the apostle. It is this theological underpinning that gives assurance to the second half of verse 5, "through Christ our consolation also increases." For just as Christ's sufferings and death are a prelude to his resurrection, Paul's own afflictions also must pave the way for consolation. In this regard, the Philippian Hymn, which depicts the same motif of suffering and vindication, is a fitting commentary on verse 5:

> But he emptied himself,
>> taking on the form of a servant,
>> becoming in human likeness.
> And after he appeared in human form,
>> he humiliated himself,
>> becoming obedient unto death —
>> even death on a cross.
> Thus, God highly exalted him
>> and bestowed on him the name above every name...
>
> (Phil 2:7–9)

Ultimately, Paul has confidence in God's consolation because of his profound conviction that Christ's death and vindication are being played out in his own ministry: as assuredly as Christ has been vindicated, his own afflictions will turn to consolation.

What Paul claims in this regard — identification with the sufferings of Christ — is not apostolic privilege but a common experience available to all, most of all the Corinthians. "If we are afflicted, it is *for the sake of your consolation and salvation;* if we are consoled, it is *for the sake of your consolation* which becomes effective as you endure the same sufferings we ourselves also suffer" (verse 6). In this verse, Paul makes two assertions about the relationship of his own afflictions and consolation to the Corinthians'. First, Paul expresses his concerns for the well-being of his converts by making clear that he has been toiling on their behalf, so that what he gains from his labors is passed on to them. Even his afflictions, dangers, and toils are all done for the sake of their "consolation and salvation." This assertion, in light of Paul's overall strategy of wooing the Corinthians back to him, is well within our expectation; elsewhere he also tells his congregations that he cares for them like a nurse to suckling babies (1 Thess 2:7–8, 11–12).

But Paul's second assertion, in the second half of verse 6, gives us pause, not the least because it seems so logically impossible to understand: "If we are consoled, it is for the sake of your consolation *which becomes effective as you endure the same sufferings we ourselves also suffer."* Paul has already mentioned earlier (verse 4) that his own consolation after having been delivered enables him to console those in every affliction, but here he stops short of saying that he could pass that consolation on to others. Rather, he insists that consolation "becomes effective" when the Corinthians themselves "endure the same sufferings" as Paul's. What Paul appears to be saying is that, if consolation turns out to be a gift from God, one receives it only when one experiences afflictions. Just as hardship is a gateway to vindication, so affliction is an occasion for divine consolation, and weakness is a prelude to power.

If that is the case, in what sense can the Corinthians be said to "endure the *same* sufferings" Paul and his colleagues have suffered? Paul is clearly not speaking of a particular occasion in which he and the Corinthians are afflicted in the same way, but rather that the Corinthians are said to share in Paul's sufferings (verse 7). The only way to understand this is to posit Christ as the middle term between Paul and his Corinthian converts. Because of their common identification with Christ's sufferings and because, in a mystical sense, every believer's suffering is also Christ's suffering, all believers are somehow involved in the "same sufferings." In other words, the mystical union with Christ extends to all believers, so that they all go through the same trials and the same tribulations that Paul has endured in his apostolic mission, and they all will receive the same deliverance and the same consolation.

It is on the basis of such a common bond between Paul and the Corinthians, maintained by their common participation in the suffering of Christ, that Paul could now issue a call to them to take part in the future deliverance: "As you also join in helping us by prayer, so that many may render thanks on our behalf for the gift of grace to us which comes as a result of the prayers of many" (verse 11). The syntax of the Greek is so convoluted that no English translation seems capable of unraveling it entirely, but the intent of the statement seems clear. What Paul asks for is prayer, prayer that would make it possible for many to give thanks to God for the grace given to Paul that delivered him from certain death (verses 9–10). In this manner, then, the traditional thanksgiving prayer makes its appearance in 2 Corinthians after all, though not as a premise to the discussion of affliction and consolation but as its conclusion. Customarily, a thanksgiving prayer functions as commendation for the love and witness of the recipients and an implicit challenge to continue in the same vein. The concluding request for prayer here functions much the same way. Regardless of what might have happened in the past, whether there is anything to be thankful for in the future depends entirely on whether and to what extent they will continue to take part in Paul's ministry.[7]

Paul in the opening salutation and blessing attempts to change the terms of the debate with his opponents. Instead of engaging in a competition based on a display of power and might, Paul focuses the attention on the human frailty and weakness of the apostle. An authentic apostle is characterized not by his impressive credentials and spiritual endowments but by the presence of God's power which shines through his human fragility. In changing the terms of the debate, Paul construes for his recipients a problem that has to do with his troubled relationship with them. This is a problem that both parties can resolve because, as Paul reminds them, they retain an indissoluble link with him through their common identification with the death and vindication of Christ. Since they are all willing participants, they must continue their support for his ministry, so that others might be able to render thanks to God for their participation in it. In naming the problem as an internal issue, moreover, Paul also implies that the solution to the problem can be sought from members of the church without having to involve his opponents who are in fact outsiders.

Cultivating Relationship with the Corinthian Church: 1:12–14

[12]For this is our boast, the witness of our conscience, that in frankness and sincerity which come from God, not in human wisdom but by the grace of God, do we behave in the world — especially for you. [13]For we write nothing to you except what you can read or what you also know. And I hope that you will know completely, [14]as you also knew us in part, that we are your boast, just as you also are ours on the day of the Lord Jesus.

Right after issuing a challenge to the Corinthians to take part in
his ministry (1:11), Paul continues to stress his bond with the
church. But this time he pursues the issue by introducing a new
element of discourse: "boast." Boasting, Paul realizes, is one of
the characteristic traits of the false apostles, for they glorify their
own spiritual prowess while diminishing that of others. Boasting is by definition self-centered and individualistic, but Paul
exploits this by applying the same procedure as before, namely,
to shift the terms of the debate in his own favor. This time, he
changes the object of boasting from his own achievements to
those of others, and in the process he solidifies the Corinthians'
bond to himself.

He begins this passage using his opponents' favorite technique of boasting: his conducts his life in "frankness and sincerity" and "not in human wisdom but by the grace of God"
(1:12). These are his usual topics, since "the grace of God" in
this connection is not significantly different from "the will of
God" by which he was called to be an apostle (1:1). But Paul
brings all these up in order to zero in on the very object of
his rhetoric, the Corinthians, by adding the phrase "especially
for you" (verse 12). This is the motivation for his behavior —
for the sake of the Corinthians. Far from self-aggrandizement,
therefore, the object of this passage is Paul's relationship to the
Corinthians, and Paul reaches it through boasting. After a brief
statement defending, somewhat self-consciously, the perspicac-
ity of his writings ("For we write nothing to you except what
you can read or what you also know," verse 13a), Paul reiterates the same point that the only true basis for boasting is the
mutually enriching relationship between himself and his converts: "We are your boast, just as you also are ours" (verse 14).
In the sense that the success of the congregation becomes part
of his achievements, Paul's boasting is no different from that
of his opponents', but Paul makes it clear that such an achievement is never divorced from the well-being of the congregation.
And that is the cause for true boasting, in accordance with the
witness of the conscience. With these preparatory remarks, Paul
begins the body of the letter proper.

Only one additional note need be sounded before moving on
to the next section, since it is a recurring theme in 2 Corinthians: that is, the eschatological dimension of "boasting." Paul
places perfect knowing "on the day of the Lord Jesus Christ"
(verse 14), i.e., the Second Coming (see 1 Cor 5:5; Phil 1:6, 10;

2:16). It is on that day when Paul's sincerity and conscience will be proven blameless, and that is the basis for his boasting about his work done among the Corinthians. True boasting is therefore confidence in the last day when one's true identity will be under scrutiny.[8]

Paul's Tortured Relationship with the Corinthians

Readers approaching the present passage will discover, explicitly for the first time, why Paul has been so careful and so subtle in constructing his opening remarks: Some of Paul's actions must have been roundly misunderstood by the Corinthians and Paul is compelled to answer to their satisfaction. From the first verses of the present passage, especially verses 15–17, where Paul mentions his canceled plans to visit Corinth, we get a sense that this is just the tip of the iceberg. As we read on, 2:2–3 holds another surprise: Paul has in fact revisited Corinth a second time after his initial sojourn there when he founded the church, but it was a visit made memorable by his having inflicted pain upon all the principals involved (verse 2). Then in 2:4, we come across Paul's mention of a letter, one which he wrote "with many tears." These are clear indications that Paul's relationship with the Corinthians has not been the happiest and it is these problems that stand in the background of the carefully composed opening.

Explanation for a Postponement
of Visit: 1:15–2:2

[15]So with this very confidence, I at first was wishing to come to you, so that you might have a double grace: [16]that is, to go to Macedonia by way of you and to come to visit you again on my way back from Macedonia, and then to be sent on to Judea by you. [17]But then, did I trifle with you because I wished it? Or, am I planning in a worldly fashion, as if to say "Yes, yes" and "No, no" all at once?

[18]But as surely as God is faithful, I swear, our word to you is not "Yes" and "No." [19]For the son of God, Jesus Christ, who was proclaimed among you through us — through me, Silvanus, and Timothy — did not become "Yes" and "No," but there was and continues to be a "Yes" in him. [20]For what

promises of God there are, are all "Yes" in him: therefore, it is through him that there is an "Amen" to God, to his glory through us. ²¹The God who confirms us with you in Christ and anointed us, ²²is also he who has stamped us with his seal and given the Spirit in our hearts as down payment.

²³I call on God as witness against me: I did not go to Corinth because I wanted to spare you — ²⁴not that we lord it over your faith but that we are fellow-workers for your joy, because you stand in faith. 2 ²For I resolved to do this: namely, not to pay you another painful visit. ²For if I pain you, who is there to cheer me up except him who is pained by me?

In spite of the overall conciliatory tone of this passage, clues abound that not all is well between Paul and the Corinthians. During the so-called "painful visit," Paul must have promised the Corinthians that he would visit them twice. This seems to be the most natural way to read the enigmatic phrase "double grace" of verse 15. He had planned to go from Ephesus to Macedonia by way of Corinth, going to Corinth by sea across the Aegean and then to Macedonia, presumably by land but also possibly by sea. On his return trip he would retrace his steps back to Corinth (1:16).

The reason for this double visit was most likely the collection for the Jerusalem church, a project that had occupied Paul ever since the Jerusalem Council (see Gal 1:10). We will consider the collection in greater detail when we come to chapters 8–9. For now it is enough to note that in 1 Cor 16:1–2 Paul had already made an attempt to complete the collection. He even dispatched Timothy to Corinth before the troubles broke out, probably for the purpose of coordinating this effort. This is why he seemed anxious to ask that the Corinthians accord Timothy the same respect and courtesy as they would himself (1 Cor 16:10–11; see also 4:17). At the writing of 1 Corinthians, before all the troubles with the church made it impossible to continue the project, he had hoped to travel to Corinth "by way of Macedonia" (16:5) and, once the collection was completed, to send it along to Jerusalem (16:3). He had not decided whether to accompany the collection to Jerusalem but would do so if it was deemed advisable (16:4).

Upon his return to Ephesus, however, he must have thought better of it and decided to cancel the visit (2 Cor 1:17; 1:23; 2:1). The reason for this change of plan can perhaps be attributed to

Timothy who must have brought back unfavorable news.[9] Thinking that the collection might be in jeopardy, Paul hastily dashed off to Corinth again in hopes of correcting the situation. Once there, however, Paul only succeeded in making matters worse. Paul had a personal confrontation with a member of the congregation, as a result of which he thought he had lost all support in Corinth and had to leave in disgrace. Before he left, though, he must have also thought that, given his tenuous relationship with the Corinthian church, the only way to pursue the collection rigorously was to visit Corinth twice: first to go to Macedonia by way of Corinth in order to supervise the continuation of the collection, then to return to Corinth on his way back from Macedonia to coordinate its completion. Evidently, he had also decided to travel to Jerusalem with the collection, a plan which he later confirms in Rom 15:25 and which, from all indications, he must have carried out as well. "Send on to" (Greek, *propempein*) became almost a technical term among Christian missionary communities in the first-century and came to mean "to support in a missionary journey" (see Rom 15:24; 1 Cor 16:6, 11; Titus 3:13; 3 John 6). This meant providing finance, escorts, (so according to Acts 20:38; 21:5), letters of recommendation (2 Cor 3:1), and other resources necessary for the trip.

Again back in Ephesus, still hurting from the bitterness of his recent visit, Paul changed his mind yet one more time. He sent "a letter of tears" in lieu of another "painful visit" (2:1; but also 1:23) in which he told the congregation in Corinth that he would keep to his original plan outlined in 1 Cor 16:5 after all. That is, he would go first to Macedonia before coming to Corinth. When Titus brought good news to Paul in Macedonia (see notes on 2:6 below) that the majority of the congregation had disciplined Paul's offender, there was nevertheless grumbling about Paul's changed travel plan. It is to those who complained — no more than a minority if Paul's representation of the situation is to be trusted — that Paul tries to answer with his rhetorical question, "Did I trifle because I wished [earlier to pay you a double visit]?" (1:17a). "Trifle" here bespeaks a lack of seriousness or responsibility, indicating a wishy-washy pattern of behavior that can only be called fickle. Such a complaint would fit in well with the portrayal of Paul as commanding a "weak presence" in spite of his strong letters (10:10; 11:5).

It is not immediately clear what exactly is the charge to which Paul's rhetorical question of 1:17 alludes: "Am I planning in a worldly fashion, as if to say 'Yes, yes' and 'No, no' all at once?"[10] Since Paul is responding to the complaint about his change of plans, he might be thought of saying both "Yes, yes" and "No, no" at the same time. In other words, it is possible that the Corinthians thought him vacillating at best, deceptive at worst. But it is also possible that some thought Paul to be an insincere flatterer, accusing him of saying "Yes, yes" to some and "No, no" to others depending on the expediency of the occasion.

Victor Furnish has suggested an intriguing hypothesis why this latest change of plan so incensed some members of the Corinthian congregation. Paul's traveling to Macedonia first could strike some Corinthians as a slight. His decision to accept financial support from the Macedonians (Phil 4:16, 18) and his refusal to accept the same from the Corinthians had already strained his relationship with the latter (2 Cor 11:8–9; see 1 Cor 9:6, 8–18).[11] Now, he seems to be, once again, giving priority to the Macedonians, and this can only heighten the competition between the Corinthians and Macedonians. Paul cannot be unaware of this competition, since he later uses it to promote the collection effort (see 2 Cor 8:1–2; 9:2–4). Under these circumstances, it is entirely possible that at least some among the Corinthian congregation accuse Paul of favoritism.[12]

Whatever might have been the exact nature of such an accusation, Paul's response in the next passage (1:18–22) would confirm his status as a masterful rhetorician. Verse 18, "As surely as God is faithful," at first reads like the start of a parenthetical statement verbally stitched on to the previous verse by a tenuous thread, "I swear, our word to you is not 'Yes' and 'No.'" But as we have seen in our discussion of the opening blessing (1:3–11), Paul's usual strategy in controversies such as this is not to confront his critics head on or to engage in a tit-for-tat dispute with them, but to appeal to God's mission in the world and, most crucially, to remind his readers of his participation in that mission. Whether it has to do with suffering or in this case a canceled visit, Paul sees a deeper theological basis lying behind. This is not to say that Paul always rationalizes his action but rather that he is so identified with his evangelizing effort that he perceives his own actions and motivations as coming from God.

Paul's approach here is no different, even if the substance of his argumentation is. He emphasizes that the Christ whom the

Corinthians had accepted was not both "Yes" and "No"; rather, "there was and continues to be" an unequivocal "Yes" of God to humanity in Christ (verse 19). Standing behind the cumbersome phrase, "was and continues to be," is the Greek perfect tense which indicates an action that happened in the past but continues to be effective in the present. Paul uses it no doubt to refer to the event of Christ's death and resurrection that continues to be efficacious in conveying God's promises to all: "What promises of God there are, they are all 'Yes' in him" (verse 20a). What Paul wants to assert, of course, is that God does not vacillate and God does not equivocate; God's statement to humanity is an eternal affirmative.

Paul immediately adds in the second half of verse 20 that not only is this the unshakable character of God, but the Corinthians are well aware of it. He reminds them that when they say "Amen" in their worship — a liturgical acclamation taken over from synagogue services meaning "may it be so" or expressing praise or blessing to God (note, e.g., 1 Cor 14:16) — they are indeed affirming the very faithfulness of God's character.

Paul's mention of a liturgical formula is not merely a capricious word play between "Yes" and "Amen"; it is actually a deliberate bid to involve the Corinthians' own religious experience in the current discussion, a move with which his readers should be familiar by now (see, e.g., 1:6–7). In pointing out the Corinthians' worship practice, Paul in effect reminds them of what made all this possible in the first place: It was "through Christ," by means of their acceptance of Christ, that the way is paved for becoming recipients of God's promises. Before their acclamation of the glory of God, therefore, there was their prior act of commitment, and before God's promises can be recognized as a "Yes," they must be met with the precondition of being "in [Christ]" (verse 20). While God is the author of an unambiguous and incontestable affirmation, Paul does not exclude his converts but includes them in the grand scheme of salvation. Paul's theological ruminations, perhaps as a result of the controversial matrix in which they are born, are never far removed from the personal and experiential. As a matter of fact, going back to verse 19, Paul does not actually say that Christ *is* God's eternal "Yes" but rather that "there was and continues to be a 'Yes' *in him*." In other words, the emphasis is placed on the human experience, not on God's offer. The other side of God's affirmation and offer to humanity is in essence humanity's experience in Christ, for it is experience that makes concrete and explicit God's original divine assertions.

But in emphasizing God's unfailing statement to the world, Paul also steadfastly emphasizes his inextricable role in conveying that statement to the Corinthians and therefore his bond to them throughout this passage. He begins by noting in verse 18 that his words to the Corinthians are not "Yes" and "No." Verse 19 makes it clear that what he means by "our word" is his proclamation of Christ among the Corinthians. For good measure he adds the names of Silvanus and Timothy just to remind his readers that they, too, are founders of the church and apostolic authorities, and that they play an indispensable role in the spiritual formation of the congregation. Even when they praise God with their Amens in services, Paul reminds them that they could do so "through us" (verse 20). The Corinthians' in-Christness, in short, owes its very existence to the mediating presence of Paul and his coworkers.

In so doing, Paul construes his relationship to the Corinthians as one of paradox. While he stresses his connection to and solidarity with his converts, he is also not above reminding them of their obligations to him. This is perhaps the reason for the peculiar mixture of involvement and aloofness, integration and separation, egalitarianism and hierarchy in verses 21–22. Paul first elevates himself and his colleagues above the Corinthians with the words, "God confirms *us with you* into Christ" (verse 21a), which establish a hierarchy of importance. "Confirm" here is a term borrowed from first-century commerce, referring to the seller's confirmation of a sale. The same is true with "down payment" of verse 22b, which was used as a guarantee or collateral that the total sum would be paid out in full in some future date. Together, these terms depict a binding transaction in which God the seller establishes the community in Christ with his seal, as well as with the giving of the Spirit as a present guarantee for the final consummation and for the perfection of all. The language most likely alludes to the baptism of the Corinthians, and it is used here to recapitulate a priority about which Paul feels the Corinthians need a gentle reminder: he and the other cofounders of the church are responsible for the baptism of the converts. It is they whom "God establishes." "With you" in this connection indicates a subordinate level of incorporation "into Christ." Once the hierarchy is affirmed, however, Paul immediately adds these words: "anointed *us*" (verse 21b), "stamped *us* with his seal" (verse 22a), and "given the Spirit in *our hearts* as down payment" (verse 22b). With this, he concedes that even though they were once masters and students, apostles, and converts, now they all merge into a united body in Christ, and they all receive the same Spirit as a guarantee of God's continual faithfulness. Chronological and logical priority of coming "into Christ" does not translate into spiritual superiority.

The same paradoxical construal also characterizes the next passage, 1:23–2:2. On the one hand, Paul is at pains to explain that he had to cancel the proposed "double visit" out of a concern for his converts. He had not wanted a repeat of his "painful visit" (2:1). There is no reason to doubt Paul's words, since he seems consistent in showing genuine care for the church he founded (see especially later 2:3–4). But what makes this statement rhetorically effective is that it comes on the heels of a statement about unity and shared commonality within the body of Christ. This theological premise inexorably leads his readers to draw the conclusion that Paul did have the Corinthians' best interest in mind when he elected not to come for the visit, and that he simply did not want to subject the congregation to another painful visit, "For if I pain you, who is there to cheer me up except him who is pained by me?" (2:2). Alternatively, if the Corinthians reject this conclusion, they would be compelled to reject the theological foundation upon which it is built. If they choose not to believe in Paul's sincerity in postponing the trip, the rhetorical logic set up in 1:18–2:2 would cast doubt on their in-Christ solidarity with Paul and company. What Paul has effectively accomplished here, therefore, is to confront his wayward converts with this choice and make their attitude towards his canceled trip into a referendum on his relationship to them in Christ.

At the same time, while relying on the persuasive power of an egalitarian theology, Paul also makes use of the authority that he feels his apostolic position affords him. In 1:23, Paul explains the canceled trip with an implicit warning: he did not come because he wanted "to spare" the Corinthians. But to spare them from what? Ostensibly Paul means the avoidance of another painful occasion (2:1). This he explicitly states: He in no way intends to "lord it over [their] faith," because he and his colleagues are their "fellow-workers" (1:24). But by stating that he does not "lord it over" the Corinthians, he is of course dropping a not-so-subtle hint that he in fact *could* lord it over them, that as their superior and father[13] he *could* discipline them or exact punishment from the offending party — even though he chooses not to on the stated ground of egalitarianism. While Paul does give the Corinthians the choice in the matter of their relationship to him, he also conveys to them that they owe this very choice to him.

Paul Forgives the Offending Party: 2:3–11

[3]And I wrote this very thing, so that when I come I would not be pained by those who should cheer me up, because I am convinced about all of you that my joy is shared by all of you. [4]For it was out of much affliction and anguish of heart that I wrote you, with many tears, not so much that you might be pained but that you might know the love which I have especially for you.

[5]If someone has caused pain, he has caused pain not to me but to some extent — not to overburden you — to all of you. [6]This very punishment dealt by the majority is enough for such a man, [7]so that you should instead forgive and console him, lest somehow such a man be consumed by excessive sorrow. [8]Therefore, I exhort you to solidify your love for him. [9]I wrote for this reason: to see if you pass the test and if you are obedient in all respects. [10]Whomever you forgive, I too forgive. Whatever I have forgiven, if I have forgiven anything, is for your sake in the presence of Christ, [11]so that we may not be taken advantage of by Satan, for we are not unaware of his schemes.

In lieu of another painful visit, Paul wrote a letter "out of much affliction and anguish of heart" and "with many tears" (2:3). In line with his stated concern for the Corinthians which was responsible for his canceled visit, here Paul reiterates the same care he has for them and then goes beyond that to declare his love for the Corinthians (2:4). Nowhere else does Paul declare his love for the Corinthians so directly and explicitly. We might question whether he in reality wrote the "letter of tears" out of love, affliction, and anguish; or whether it is more likely that the letter was issued from rage. If we are to infer from the ensuing action taken by the Corinthians to discipline the offender (verse 6), we can assume that the letter must have conveyed threats and warnings rather than affections. Nevertheless, there is no denying that Paul's affection for the Corinthians is genuine and is deeply grounded in his conviction that he and his converts are closely identified in sufferings and in joy. His perception of his identification with them is so close he could boldly declare, "My joy is shared by all of you" (2:3). Paul is convinced that when the offender caused him pain, he has also caused pain to all the Corinthians (2:5). Such identification language recalls his earlier statement that he and his Corinthian converts share the same sufferings, because both identify with Christ's sufferings (1:6–7).

Paul does not reveal the identity of the transgressor or what exactly the offense was. The language of 2:5–8, 11; 7:12 indicates that Paul has a specific person in mind, but who this "someone" (verse 5) is remains a mystery. Judged by the masculine used in verses 6, 7 ("such a man") — and the fact that the congregation had the authority to discipline him even though the nature of that punishment also remains in the dark (verse 6) — he must have been a man from within the church. Classical writers ranging from church fathers to early twentieth-century commentators took him to be the incestuous man described in 1 Cor 5:1–5 and, correspondingly, understood 1 Corinthians to be the "letter of tears." But there is little chance that this could be the case. There is no evidence in our passage that the offense was sexual; in fact, according to 7:12, Paul describes *himself* as the one who has been wronged by the offender, which makes it highly unlikely that the offense of 2 Corinthians was sexual in nature. Moreover, Paul condemns the immoral man mentioned in 1 Cor 5:1 to Satan, thereby excommunicating him from the congregation; here, however, Paul advises that the offender be restored to fellowship after he has been punished.

If the offender here is not the man of 1 Corinthians 5, then there is no firm basis for determining what the transgression was. Some have speculated that it might have been a public slander against Paul.[14] In the absence of a better alternative, the theory at least helps highlight important features in this controversy. It was an offense against Paul himself, as we have seen in 7:12, and not against the whole congregation. That is why in 2:5 Paul feels that he himself needs to make an explicit association between this man's misdeed and its effect on the whole community. This man has caused pain not only to himself but — "not to overburden you" — also to the whole assembly. At the same time, the offense must have been of a public nature, because Paul assumes the knowledge of it among his readers to such an extent that he need not belabor the details. Only such a public scenario would lead Paul to think that an individual so hurt could represent the whole congregation (2:5), and that the church could legitimately "forgive and console" the transgressor (2:7).

Even though a single individual was responsible for the offense, Paul does not think the Corinthians should be exculpated, however. He holds the whole community responsible, saying in 2:9, "I wrote [the letter of tears] for this reason: to see if you *pass the test* and if you are obedient in all respects." Again in 7:12 he says, "Although I wrote to you, it was not on account of the one who has done the wrong or on account of the one who has been wrong, but in order that *your eagerness for us* might be made manifest to you before God." From these statements, we get a sense that Paul was equally irked by the Corinthians' lack of demonstrable support for him when he was first insulted. One could further postulate that perhaps after his departure, the Corinthians at first seemed unwilling to discipline the offender. If this is the case — that the offense was some public effrontery against Paul and that the Corinthians were complicit in some way — then the offense must have been more than a personal slight, but a challenge to Paul's apostolic authority and his standing in the congregation. In all likelihood, the offense might have reflected a struggle for leadership between Paul and the unnamed offender in the community, one in which its members must decide whom they will follow. At least this is how Paul has represented the problem to his readers. These events cast doubts in Paul's mind about the Corinthians' loyalty to him, and he decided to write the letter of tears to test them. Like the canceled trip before, his row with an individual member again raises the sensitive question of his relationship to the community.

The tearful letter did achieve the salutary effect. Forced to choose between the offender and Paul, the congregation, at least "a majority" of them, cast their lots with Paul, and, to show their sincerity, they exacted some "punishment" on the errant man. For Paul, the real issue has less to do with the offense itself or the offender, and more to do with what impact it has on his relation with the Corinthian church. He does not comment on the repentance of the offender and does not even raise the possibility of reconciling with him personally. It was enough for Paul's purpose that *the congregation* have finally shown support for him and that they have responded favorably to his overture for reconciliation. Feeling consoled and secure once again, Paul can now afford to show his magnanimity towards the offender, pleading on his behalf for leniency: "You should instead forgive and console him, lest somehow such a man be consumed by excessive sorrow. Therefore, I exhort you to solidify your love for him" (2:7–8). The Corinthians' forgiveness of the man paves the way for Paul's own forgiveness of him, so that he can now reaffirm his solidarity with the congregation: "Whomever you forgive, I too forgive" (2:10). Paul's focal concern in this letter is none other than his relationship to the congregation.

Travelogue:
2:12–13; 7:5–7

2 ¹²When I came to Troas to preach the gospel of Christ — for a door was opened for me in the Lord — ¹³I did not have peace in my spirit because I did not find Titus my brother, but after I said goodbye to them, I left for Macedonia.

7 ⁵Even when we came into Macedonia, we had no peace but were afflicted everywhere: Battles without; fears within. ⁶But God, consoler of the lowly, consoled us with the arrival of Titus — ⁷not only with his arrival but also with the consolation with which he was consoled about you, when he announced to us concerning your longing, your mourning, your zeal for me — so much so that I rejoiced still more.

Paul's travel narrative to Troas and Macedonia, where he waited for but did not meet Titus (2:12–13), is unceremoniously broken off in mid-sentence and does not resume until five chapters later, in 7:5. In between is a long, elaborate exegetical discussion (2:14–7:4) that occasionally packs a polemical edge but otherwise has little to do with what comes before or after. When the travel narrative does pick up again in 7:5, Titus does meet Paul in Macedonia with the welcome news that the Corinthians have had a change of heart (7:6–7). What comes next is a passage (7:8–16) that goes over many of the same themes we have already

encountered in 2:5–11: the letter of tears (7:8; compare with
2:3–4, 9), the offender (7:12; compare with 2:5, 6), "vengeance"
presumably referring to the punishment meted out to the offender (7:11; compare with 2:6), and Paul's commendation for
the Corinthians' having proved themselves (7:11; compare with
2:9). But it makes no reference to the long intervening section
of 2:14–7:4.[15] As we will see in the next chapter, 2:14–7:4 is a
polemic piece written with outside missionaries in mind. By contrast, the problem that preoccupies Paul up to 2:13 is strictly his
relationship with the congregation; outside agitators, if they are
present in Corinth at this time, do not come into the purview of
Paul's rhetoric. These are strong indications that this intervening section (2:14–7:4) must have belonged to a different letter,
one which reflects a more controversial phase of Paul's relationship with the Corinthians.[16] For this reason, our discussion of
Paul's travelogue will proceed directly to 7:5–16, where Paul's
letter of reconciliation comes to a logical conclusion, and will
treat 2:14–7:4 as a separate letter in the next chapter.

The travelogue on the surface seems like a distraction from
the sustained gesture toward reconciliation, as documented in
2:5–11 and 7:8–13, but is in fact part and parcel of Paul's continual attempt at cementing his relationships with the Corinthians.
The use of travel narrative is one of Paul's favorite literary techniques to cultivate relationship with his congregation. The first
instance of this in the extant Pauline corpus can be found in
1 Thessalonians, a letter sent to a church of which Paul is no
doubt very fond. He praises the Thessalonians for being a model
of faith to all the Macedonian and Achaian churches (1 Thess
1:7) and for receiving the gospel and suffering the consequences
(2:13–14). He describes his relationship to the Thessalonians at
times as a nurse (2:7) or father (2:11) to his children, at times
as an orphan to his missing parents (2:17). In effusive language
he declares: "So deeply do we care for you that we are determined to share with you not only the gospel of God but also
our own selves, because you have become very dear to us" (2:8;
NRSV), "You are our glory and joy!" (2:20). To convey this affection to the Thessalonians, Paul structures an elaborate travel
narrative taking up nearly half of the letter in which he recounts events in Philippi leading up to the conversion of the
Thessalonians (2:1–2), the founding of the church (2:3–12), his
departure from Thessalonica and his deep yearning to return
(2:17–20). But since he could not return immediately ("Satan

blocked our way," 2:18), Paul goes on to tell his readers that he sent Timothy from Athens back to strengthen those being persecuted (3:1–5) and found relief only when Timothy returned with the good news that the new converts in Thessalonica had stood firm (3:6). Such a presentation paints a picture of profound concern and deep longing for the church. Even though Paul is constantly on the road and in spite of his physical absence from the congregation, his heart aches to be with his beloved children, and he would return once an opportunity presents itself. What Paul hopes to achieve by this is, of course, closer union and solidarity with his congregation, even in his travels. He dispatches his emissary Timothy and the letter of 1 Thessalonians itself to the church to accomplish the same thing: to establish and realize his apostolic presence in their midst.[17] But the travelogue also functions in a less tangible, more imaginative way. By sharing with the church what Paul has gone through, the narrative draws the readers into itself and induces them to identify with the absent apostle. The notion that a congregation experiences the same joy and suffering as Paul is already familiar to us; the travelogue pushes that one step further by making this identification into a participation in the Pauline mission.

Paul probably intends to accomplish similar goals with his travel narrative in 2 Corinthians. Paul tells his readers in 2:12 that he came to Troas because of an opportunity to preach the gospel. But Paul was so preoccupied with the controversy brewing in Corinth that he had no peace. Titus, whom he had sent to Corinth earlier, possibly to deliver the "letter of tears," had yet to return and there was no news about the reception of his stern missive. In the midst of his anxiety, he had to move on to Macedonia (2:13). Paul describes his experience in Macedonia as beset with afflictions (7:5), but nevertheless God consoled him (7:6). Finally, Titus arrived in Macedonia, and Paul was again consoled, this time by the good news that the Corinthians had reacted positively to the letter. By recounting his travel from Troas to Macedonia Paul wants to convey to the Corinthians his extreme anxiety for them. Even in the midst of his evangelistic work in Troas, he had the affairs in Corinth constantly in his heart, and the recounting of his itinerary serves to add vividness to this picture of anxiety. Thus, by sending Titus back and forth between himself and Corinth, Paul was able to establish his presence in the church by proxy.

But it is possible that Paul also wants to remind the Corinthians of their deep bonds with him. Paul does not mention why he left Troas, but it was clearly not because Titus had not returned. If Acts 16:7–11 chronicles the same visit, Paul's stay in this prominent Asian city was indeed brief. In 2 Cor 2:13, Paul does not elaborate on his ministry there in spite of an initial openness to the gospel. This leads one to suspect that perhaps the mission had not fared as well as hoped. It is also possible that Troas was where Paul had "the affliction we experienced in Asia" (1:8), though one cannot be sure.[18] The language of affliction and consolation in 7:5–7 cannot but be intended to recall the similar language of the opening blessing (1:3–7), where Paul uses affliction and consolation as the twin themes to convey to the Corinthians that they suffer the same sufferings, and are consoled with the same consolation, as he was. His travelogue in 7:5–7, therefore, is the continuation of the theme that the Corinthians have suffered the same afflictions as Paul himself experienced in Macedonia. He was consoled by the news brought back by Titus; it was only because of "the consolation with which [Titus] was consoled about you" (7:7). The Corinthians share with Paul the same affliction and the same joy, and both are bound up in the same ministry.

Reconciliation and Renewed Confidence: 7:8–16

[8]Because even though I pained you with the letter I do not regret it — though I did regret it; I see that letter did pain you, though only for a moment. [9]Now I rejoice, not because you have been pained but because you have been pained for the sake of repentance. For you have been pained by God, and so you have not been hurt by us. [10]For the pain which comes from God produces repentance for the sake of salvation without regret, but the pain from the world produces death. [11]For see what earnestness this pain according to God has produced: such defense, such indignation, such alarm, such longing, such zeal, such vengeance. In every thing you have proved yourselves to be blameless in this matter. [12]Then, although I wrote to you, it was not on account of the one who has done the wrong or on account of the one who has been wronged, but in order that your earnestness for us might be

made manifest to you before God. ¹³This is why we were and
continue to be consoled.

In addition to our consolation, we rejoiced still more at the
joy of Titus, because his spirit has been set to rest by all of you.
¹⁴For if I have somehow boasted to him on your behalf, I was
not put to shame. But, just as I spoke all things to you in truth,
so our boast to Titus turned out also to be true. ¹⁵His heart
goes out to you all the more, even as he remembers the obedience of all of you, how you received him with respect and
trembling. ¹⁶I rejoice because I have every confidence in you.

With this discussion of solidarity in place (2:12–13; 7:5–7), Paul
returns to dealing with the aftermath caused by the letter of
tears, but here Paul seems ready to put the whole unpleasant
affair behind him and to move on with the positive outcome
effected by the letter. We have already seen in our discussion
of 2:5–11 that Paul construes the problem not as one between
himself and the offender but as one between himself and the Corinthians. Paul continues this tack, but now he shifts the accent
to the Corinthians' relationship to God, content to play midwife
to the Corinthians' learning experience. The whole ordeal, according to Paul, is a testing from God that eventually produces
virtue and confidence.

Paul refers again to the letter of tears in verse 8, but unlike
before, he emphasizes not his own anguish but what effect it has
had on the Corinthians. Paul acknowledges that the letter might
have "pained" his readers, but he does this only to create an
opening to make a distinction between "pain which comes from
God" and "pain of the world" in verses 9–11. What Paul refers to
by "pain which comes from God" is probably the ordeals which
God permits humanity to suffer for the sake of building character (verse 11) and "salvation" (verse 10a), whereas "pain from
the world" is its opposite (verse 10b). Because the Corinthians
have repented (verses 9, 10), Paul feels justified in concluding
that the pain they have endured has been divinely ordained.
Otherwise, Paul says, how else could one explain the presence of
"such defense, such indignation, such alarm, such longing, such
zeal, such vengeance" (verse 11)? Each of these is most likely a
generalized feature of a specific instance that Paul has witnessed
in the Corinthians. All this allows Paul to say in verse 12 that
"I wrote . . . in order that your earnestness for us might be made
manifest *to you* before God." At bottom, Paul contends that the

actions the Corinthians have taken are purely a matter between them and God. And if this controversy has been a testing (see 2:9), "In every thing you have proved yourselves to be blameless in the matter" —also before God (7:11). Paul can conclude that he is consoled (verse 13a), because the Corinthians are again right with God.

The theme of consolation allows Paul to focus his attention next on Titus and his role in the collection (7:13b–16). Titus brought the good news back from Corinth but is also scheduled to return to Corinth to finish with the collection business (8:6, 16, 23; for collection for the Jerusalem church, see chapter 5). To pave the way for his return, Paul prepares this transitional section, stressing Titus's recent role in quelling the unrest (verse 13b), his compassion and concerns for the Corinthians (verse 15a), and the Corinthians' reception of him (verse 15b). In so doing, Paul also reminds his readers that Titus goes to Corinth as *his* emissary. He had already boasted to Titus of the Corinthians; it has proven to be true in this last visit and Paul was not put to shame (verse 14). For good measure, Paul tells his readers that Titus "remembers the *obedience* of all of you" (verse 15). Obedience, in fact, is precisely what Paul had asked for earlier when he wrote the letter of tears (2:9). Titus, in other words, has experienced everything Paul has experienced and knows what Paul knows; he therefore must be received as Paul's representative. Paul ends chapter 7 with an exuberant exclamation, "I rejoice because I have every confidence in you" (verse 16).

*Chapter 4*_____

The Characteristic of Authentic Ministry: 2:14–7:4

These chapters form the core of 2 Corinthians, yet they do not seem to cohere into any readily discernible pattern. Paul appears to jump from topic to topic, treating the new covenant in one chapter (3:1–18), recounting his own afflictions in the next (especially 4:7–18), calling for reconciliation in still another (5:11–21). To see what gathers these chapters into a thematic unity, it is important to note at the outset that Paul developed all these arguments in the context of controversy. In contrast to the previous section which ends on a conciliatory note (see especially 2:5–11), here Paul seems much more disputatious. He makes a sharp distinction between himself and some itinerant preachers from the outside whom he disparagingly calls "peddlers of the word of God" (2:17). He sardonically derides the Corinthians for even thinking of asking him for documentation of his credentials (3:1). And he beseeches the Corinthians, almost plaintively (5:20), to be reconciled to him. Regardless of whether Paul is attacking his enemies or defending himself against their criticisms, one must read this central portion of 2 Corinthians with an eye on Paul's preoccupation with his opponents.

At heart, Paul wants his readers to discern the true character of an authentic ministry, so that they could resist the seduction of outside missionaries. Ostentatious and extravagant displays of personal strengths have led the Corinthians to the mistaken conclusion that the essence of ministry consists of power and might. While authentic ministry does involve power and might, they are *God's*, not the minister's. An authentic minister of the gospel is characterized, ironically, not by power but by weakness — weakness that makes it necessary for one to rely totally on God.

What Is Authentic Ministry and
Who Is Equal to It? 2:14–16

[14]Thanks be to God, who always leads us in a triumphal procession in Christ and who makes known through us the fragrance of the knowledge about him everywhere. [15]For we are the aroma of Christ to God among those being saved and those perishing. [16]To some, this is a fragrance from death to death, to others a fragrance from life to life. Who is competent to discharge such responsibilities?

Readers might be misled by the imagery of triumphal procession in 2:14a into thinking that Paul is depicting himself taking part in a victorious procession. While that is true, Paul's part in the procession is not what one might think. "To lead a procession" translates the Greek verb *thriambeuein*, which takes as its direct object *captives, the vanquished,* not the victorious generals or viceroys. In accordance with Roman customs, the victorious general leads his vanquished foes, with their leaders first in tow, in a parade through the entrance to a major city and in a major thoroughfare between cheering crowds, as a public display of civic celebration. The procession would normally end in the execution of the prisoners or their representatives. The first-century writer Plutarch records one such famous incident after the defeat of the allied forces of Mark Antony and Cleopatra. Augustus insisted on taking Cleopatra in a procession through Rome, but Cleopatra, unable to face such public humiliation, chose instead to take her own life by the bite of an asp before Mark Antony's tomb. Augustus had the last word, however. In his victory procession to the gate of the temple, he displayed a likeness of Cleopatra with an asp wrapped around her.[1]

Accordingly, in 2:14, Paul depicts himself as being led in a triumphal procession as a captive, not as a victorious general. He puts himself in the position of a captive who has no will of his own, no say on what his future might be, his life all but spent, his fate depending on the vagaries of his captor's whims. This is how he characterizes his call to be an apostle and his mission in general. He is held captive as a result of God's revelation to him

(Gal 1:15; 1 Cor 15:8–11), as an itinerant missionary traveling from place to place, he is under constant affliction and danger (2 Cor 1:4–6, 8–10; 4:8–12; 11:23–33), he goes where the Spirit leads him but otherwise has no will of his own (see, e.g., Gal 2:2). And Paul is keenly aware that his life is no longer his own (Gal 2:19–20; 2 Cor 5:14–15). This is what he means when he says that it is God "who through us makes known the fragrance of the knowledge about him everywhere" (verse 14b).

Paul's uses of "fragrance" or "aroma" in verses 14b–16 might allude to the image of a sacrifice in which aromatic smoke from a burnt offering rises up to God from the altar. Paul makes the sacrificial imagery even stronger by calling himself "the aroma of Christ to God" (verse 15), thereby suggesting that Christ is the sacrificial victim and he himself is the smoke that rises up to God. Reference to a sacrifice would fit in well with the image of a triumphal procession, since it was as much a religious festival as it was a spectacular cavalcade designed to inculcate civic pride. Besides affirming the people's allegiance and perhaps gratitude to the victorious general, it was also an occasion for rendering thanksgiving to the deities.

But it is also possible that Paul has in mind here the image of Lady Wisdom, *Sophia*, a mythical being who is a personification of the wisdom of God in Jewish tradition. She was brought forth as God's first act of creation (Prov 8:22–31) and, as the consort of God, herself participated in creation (Prov 8:30). In the Hellenistic-Jewish writing *Wisdom of Solomon*, she is God's personal emissary, leaving the heavenly realm to seek lovers of wisdom but unfortunately finding no one. Disappointed, she returns to heaven.[2] Also relevant to Paul's language here are two passages from the book of *Ben Sirach* in which fragrance and aroma are combined in praise of *Sophia:*

> Like cassia and camel's thorn I [i.e., Wisdom] gave forth
>   *aromatic perfume,*
> and like choice myrrh I spread my *fragrance,*
> like galbanum, onycha, and stacte,
> and the like *odor* of incense in the tent
>   (24:15; adapted from NRSV).

> Listen to me [i.e., Wisdom], my faithful children
> and blossom like a rose growing by a stream of water.
> Send out *aromatic fragrance* like incense,
> and put forth blossoms like a lily,

Scatter the *fragrance*, and sing a hymn of praise;
bless the Lord for all his works

(39:13–14; adapted from NRSV).

The second of these passages provides an especially close parallel to Paul, since it describes Sophia exhorting her "faithful children" to "send out aromatic fragrance" and "scatter the fragrance." This is exactly what Paul says when he calls himself and fellow-missionaries the "aroma of Christ." But if Sophia indeed stands in the background of Paul's thought in our passage, it is Christ who is compared to her; Paul reserves for himself only a secondary, derivative role, content to be her child. Christ remains the primary focus in Paul's view. The distinction between Christ and Paul thus makes explicit what is only implicitly stated in verse 14, that God makes known to the world knowledge of him *through* the apostle. In the midst of proclaiming the weightiness of his message, Paul carefully distinguishes between it and the messengers who carry it.

Whether Paul envisages here a sacrificial or wisdom image, both are similar to a triumphal procession in one crucial respect: Paul the apostle plays a secondary role to God in the cosmic drama that unfolds in the revelation of Christ. As a captive in a victory celebration which eventually leads to his own execution, he stresses that victory over life and power to determine death, glory, and honor all reside with God, while his own prerogatives and initiatives, are completely denuded. "Fragrance of the knowledge about him" conveys the notion that he is but a conduit to God's message, which is knowledge about him through Christ; otherwise he has no message of his own.

When Paul diminishes his own significance, he is, of course, following his subtle rhetorical strategy against his opponents. By subordinating the role of a missionary to God, Paul in effect puts himself and his opponents on equal footing and thus changes the criteria by which an authentic minister is to be evaluated. His opponents claim superhuman strengths and impressive credentials, but Paul argues that all these qualities play but a subservient role in the proclamation of the salvific message. If the Corinthians are seduced by these itinerant preachers, they are likely to miss out on the main event. Paul stresses his own personal inadequacies, but these are precisely qualities that transform someone into a suitable conduit for the message of the gospel to come through unimpeded. Not personal prowess but purity of the medium channels the unalloyed word of God to its hearers. Instead of matching strength for strength with his opponents — if he were to do so, he would fall prey to their traps — Paul questions the necessity of personal merit, thus changing the terms of the debate altogether. As a result, the question from now on is no longer "What credentials must we enumerate to prove our worthiness?" but "Why enumerate credentials at all?"

Responses to God's message vary: Some see it as "a fragrance from life to life"; others see it as a fragrance "from death to death" (verse 16a). Paul is clearly not espousing a doctrine of predestination here. Rather, he is depicting the burden that weighs on every preacher by noting the dire consequences that come with the message. Reception or rejection of the gospel are life-and-death decisions; no one, therefore, can take the task of preaching the gospel lightly. "Who can actually hope to be competent enough to discharge such awesome responsibilities?" (verse 16b).[3] The rhetorical force of the question demands an answer, *"No one!* Not his opponents and certainly not the captive who is himself about to lose his life!"

God Equips Ministers
for a Ministry of Glory: 2:17–3:6

2 [17]For we are not like the many peddlers of God's word, but we speak out of purity which comes from God, before God, in Christ. 3 Are we beginning again to recommend ourselves? Surely we do not need, as some do, letters of recommendation to you or from you, do we? [2]You yourselves are our letter, written in our hearts, known and read by all people, [3]for you show that you are a letter of Christ, served by us, inscribed not with ink but with the Spirit of the living God, not on tablets of stone but on tablets of human hearts.

[4]We have such a confidence through Christ before God, [5]not that we are so competent by ourselves that we reckon anything would come out of ourselves, but our capability comes from God, [6]who also made us into competent ministers of a new covenant — a new covenant based not on the letter but on the Spirit. For the letter kills, but the Spirit makes alive.

This passage at first reads like a diversion from the question concerning competency which ends the last section. But Paul is in fact answering specific questions that were prompted by an unfavorable comparison with the impressive-looking newcomers, questions that ultimately raised doubts about his fitness, his adequacy, his competence to be an apostle. Right after he outlines the proper responsibilities of an authentic minister in the previous section, it is of course natural to answer how he himself measures up to these standards. But in the course of responding to these questions, Paul also introduces his next theme: the new covenant. This new theme is to determine his discussion in the rest of chapter 3.

From Paul's rhetoric in 2:17–3:3 we can surmise that he is concerned with answering two specific charges against him: namely, his refusal to accept financial support from the Corinthians for his ministry and his lack of letters of recommendation to document his credentials. Both became issues, most likely because they are the very strengths of his opponents. From early Christian writings, including Paul's letters, we know it was common for first-century preachers to be supported in their ministry and, conversely, congregations were eager to finance them. This reciprocal relationship was part of the Roman patron-client system through which wealthy patrons contracted artisans, politicians, teachers, and all who could provide useful service to their households. Since early congregations met in private homes, it was only a matter of time before the same patron-client relationship found its way into the burgeoning churches. Well-to-do congregations, headed by patriarchs of the house, naturally wanted to extend financial support to those who ministered among them.[4]

Those whom Paul calls derisively "peddlers of God's word" (2:17) are such itinerant preachers as entered into a client relationship with the Corinthian patrons. Paul, for his part, had steadfastly refused this financial patronage offered by the Corinthians. Judged from 1 Cor 9:6–18, this refusal was interpreted by the Corinthians as a reflection of impure motives. To make matters worse, Paul evidently did receive money from other congregations, notably the Philippians and Macedonians (see Phil 4:16, 18; 2 Cor 11:9). This could not but be perceived by the Corinthians as inconsistency. It is this controversy that stands behind Paul's complaint in 12:13, "How is it that you have been made inferior *to the other churches*, except that I did not burden you financially? Forgive me this wrong!" As we saw in the last chapter, this perceived slight might have also been responsible for their questioning the motive behind Paul's changed itinerary (1:15–17). To all this, Paul can offer no rebuttal except to present his pure motive. The word "purity" is the opposite of "mixture," and here it means "sincerity." With undaunted clarity, he speaks "from God, before God, in Christ" (2:17).

The second charge has to do with Paul's lack of letters of recommendation. The Corinthians' demand for them so exasperated Paul that he protests, "Are we beginning again to recommend ourselves? Surely we do not need, *as some do*, letters of recommendation to you or from you, do we?" (3:1). In an age of poor communication, letters of recommendation gave communities in far-flung cities an effective means of maintaining a network of social and commercial relations. By way of introduction afforded by such a letter, travelers to a new city or novices in a new trade gained the confidence of a new community and entrance into them. Traveling missionaries in early Christianity also made extensive use of the tool, and these outside itinerant preachers most likely arrived in Corinth carrying impressive letters of recommendation from highly placed authorities as a way of insinuating themselves into the church. Paul himself was not averse to following the same convention: he sent a letter of recommendation on behalf of Pheobe to the church in Rome, a congregation unfamiliar to him but in which he felt he had standing based on reputation alone (see Romans 16, especially verse 1). What he objects to is that he, founder of the Corinthian church and father to his converts there, is compelled to produce the kind of document giving external validation that only outsiders should need.

The use of "again" perhaps points to a time when Paul *did* have to recommend himself to the Corinthian congregation, presumably when Paul first came to Corinth to win converts. But Paul reminds them that their relationship has gone beyond that stage, and surely he would not need to prove himself all over again to the Corinthians. Even more absurd would be to ask Paul to submit a letter of recommendation from another community. There is no evidence from any of the extant letters that the Corinthians actually demanded such a reference. In all likelihood Paul reduces the situation to such an absurdity in order to drive home a point. There can be no need for outside references as far as Paul's relationship to the Corinthians is concerned.

Paul's ministry in the church speaks for itself. It is something all churches can read and bear witness to. It is already a part of his portfolio, his *résumé*, documenting his accomplishments. Paul therefore could conclude, "*You yourselves* are our letter, written in our[5] hearts, known and read by all people" (3:2).

So far, Paul has been using his language metaphorically, but his imagery soon takes a sharp allegorical turn. To compare Paul's accomplishments in the Corinthian church, well known to all, to a letter of recommendation in a metaphorical sense, is a simple comparison because they help document Paul's credentials; their collective witness is something Paul could produce at any time for all to peruse. But Paul's words in verse 3 go beyond that simple comparison: "For you show that you are a letter of Christ, ministered by us, inscribed not with ink but with the Spirit of the living God, not on tablets of stone but on tablets of human hearts." The precise meaning of the phrase, "letter of Christ," is left unexpressed until we read in what way this letter has been written in the first of two antithetical statements: "not with ink but with a Spirit of a living God." By using this phrase, Paul helps the Corinthians recall, by association, the outpouring of the Spirit and the attending miracles that formed part of the their conversion experience. In Gal 3:2–3 Paul alludes to such a scene: "Does [God] who *supplies you with the Spirit* and *works miracles* among you do so on the basis of the law of faith that comes from hearing?" But if this is the case, the Corinthians are a "letter of Christ" no longer in the metaphorical sense; they are experientially a document penned by the Spirit for all to read.

Paul establishes this literalism, because he wants to introduce a new set of associations with his next antithetical statement: "not on tablets of stone but on tablets of human hearts." Earlier in verse 2, Paul calls the Corinthian congregation a letter of recommendation written in the hearts, but there Paul intends nothing more profound than the contention that Paul's accomplishments in Corinth are public credentials for all to see. Here, however, Paul contrasts "heart" to "stone," thus calling attention to the heart as the new medium on which the eschatological Spirit writes its new scripts. This contrast between heart and stone is the major point of departure in the discussion of the new covenant which, according to Jer 31:31–34, will govern God's renewed relationship with the people of God in the last days:

The days are surely coming, says the Lord, when I will make a new covenant with the house of Israel and the house of Judah. It will not be like the covenant that I made with their ancestors when I took them by the hand to bring them out of the land of Egypt — a covenant that they broke, though I was their husband, says the Lord. But this is the covenant that I will make with the house of Israel after those days, says the Lord; I will put my law within them, and I will write it on their hearts; and I will be their God, and they shall be my people. No longer shall they teach one another, or say to each other, "Know the Lord," for they shall all know me, from the least of them to the greatest, says the Lord; for I will forgive their iniquity, and remember their sin no more (NRSV).

"The covenant that I made with their ancestors when I took them … out of the land of Egypt" is an unmistakable reference to the Mosaic covenant on Mount Sinai. This, in Jeremiah's prophecy, is contrasted to the "new covenant" which God will establish with the new people. Unlike the former covenant in which the law was given on stone tablets external to human experience, the new covenant stipulates that the law will be written in the hearts of the new people. Paul, like many other first-century apocalyptic Jews, thought that this prophecy would be fulfilled only in the end time. But now that the gentiles are experiencing the outpouring of the Spirit at their conversion, this must evidence a fulfillment of this promise.

For Paul the end time has arrived, even though the final consummation is yet to take place. According to traditional Jewish apocalyptic views, this age would end and the age to come will be established as the just reign of God. The presence of the Spirit of God, however, is proof to Paul that the age to come has indeed been inaugurated even as this age continues to run its course. He expresses the notion of the overlapping of the two aeons in 1:22, where the Spirit is called a "first installment" (Greek, *arrabōn*) that guarantees the final consummation. Also in 5:5, where the same word is used (translated as "guarantee" in the NRSV), he again calls the Spirit a "down payment" on the total promised pledge. While the present evil age is being phased out as a result of Christ's death and resurrection, it has not been completely overturned. By the same token, the age to come, the expected age of the Messiah, has already started. The granting of the Spirit upon all and the believers' experience of it is indication that the new age is here, even though the whole creation still yearns for its final consummation and for the new creation to be perfected. Thus Paul deftly turns a demand for recommendation letters into an opening for a discussion of the new covenant.

This groundwork established, Paul returns to the question of competency in 2:16, "Who is competent to discharge such responsibilities?" which he weaves into his discussion of the new covenant. "Competence" (Greek, *hikanōtes*) is the ability to accomplish the task or demand at hand, and the verb "to make sufficient, to qualify" (Greek, *hikanoun*) also means "to empower, to authorize." The verb is used in Joel 2 to describe the conditions of withstanding the frightful portents on the day of judgment, a day so terrifying that the prophet cries in despair, "What can *endure* it?" (NRSV). If Joel stands in the background, then Paul's question in 2:16 may reflect the same eschatological sense. The required answer implied by this rhetorical question is that no one can be competent by himself to serve as an authentic minister of the gospel. Here, in the context of the new covenant, Paul can give a definitive reply. "Who is equal to the awesome task demanded by the new covenant? No one!" What makes Paul and his fellow missionaries equal to the job, however, and what enables them to discharge their responsibilities faithfully, is God's competence. God alone, not Paul or anyone else, can empower the apostle for the task ahead (3:5–6).

As a result of the new covenant, Paul and his associates have reason to have confidence, but this is not confidence in one's innate abilities but in God's authority and power: We have such a confidence through Christ before God" (3:4). "Confidence" in the first-century Hellenistic world implied an inner disposition of quiet assurance. Among Jewish and early Christian authors, the word was used to denote an ability to speak boldly before God in the last day.[6] It is this eschatological flavor that Paul wishes to instill with the use of this concept both here and in verse 12.

What God has equipped Paul and his fellow missionaries for is to become ministers of a new covenant (3:6), to which the stone-heart contrast in 3:3 has already alluded. But note the contrast here is *not* between a new covenant and the old, as if Paul and his fellow-missionaries depicted themselves as ministers of a new covenant and thereby implied that their silent opponents lurking in the background are guardians of a leftover, old covenant. This was the position of an overwhelming majority of older commentators, who took verse 6 as Paul's declaration of a decisive break from Judaism. According to this line of interpretation, Christianity represents the new covenant galvanized by Spirit and freedom, while Judaism is still mired in the old covenant, which is characterized by the letter of the law and legalism. This is also the origin of the understanding of the letter-spirit contrast as one between literalism and inner essence.

This interpretation of verse 6, however, cannot be farther from Paul's intention. First of all, the early Christians did not have a monopoly on the term; the Qumran sectarians used the term to describe their own community (*Damascus Document* 6:19; 18:21 [=19:33–34]; 20:12; *Habakkuk Pesher* 2:3 [conjectured]). Secondly, Paul does *not* in fact explicitly contrast the new covenant with the old. Paul does not even mention the old covenant in this connection, even though he clearly implies it. Modern readers, from a perspective acquired after the breakup between Christians and Jews towards the end of the first century, would have to read such an old-new contrast into the text. Instead, Paul contrasts between "letter" and "Spirit," both of which are grammatically dependent on and thus qualify "new covenant." In other words, the bone of contention between Paul and his opponents was actually *what type of new covenant* the early Christian communities represent: Is it a covenant characterized by "letter" or by "Spirit"? It is far easier to recognize that Paul's opponents are themselves missionaries concerned with the propagation of the faith and that they likely considered themselves to be ministers of a new covenant. What Paul and his opponents cannot agree on is whether the new covenant is to be defined by "letter" or "Spirit." What Paul has in mind in using letter and Spirit is a contrast between reliance on the Mosaic law and on the Spirit which all believers experience in their conversion experience. This Paul develops more fully in the rest of chapter 3.

The Ministry of Glory:
3:7–18

3 **7**If the ministry of death, engraved in letters on stone, came about in splendor, so that the children of Israel could not gaze intently into the face of Moses on account of the glory on his face — though this glory is being made obsolete — [8]how much more resplendent will the ministry of the Spirit be? [9]For if there was glory in the ministry of condemnation, how much more abundant is the glory of the ministry of righteousness! [10]That which had splendor has become no splendor at all in this regard on account of the surpassing glory. [11]If that which is being annulled came in glory, how much more does that which abides permanently come in glory!

[12]With such hope, we behave with great boldness — [13]not like Moses who put a cover over his face so that the Israelites would not gaze at the end of what was being annulled. [14]But their minds were hardened, for even to this very day the same veil remains upon their reading of the old covenant — it is not unveiled because it is in Christ that it is abolished. [15]But until today, whenever Moses is read, a veil covers their heart. [16]"Whenever one turns to the Lord, the veil is removed." [17]Now "the Lord" is the Spirit; where the Spirit of the Lord is, there is freedom. [18]We, all of us, with unveiled faces, beholding as in a mirror the glory of the Lord, are being transformed into the same image, from one degree of glory into another, just as it is from "the Lord," the Spirit.

This difficult passage is full of convoluted arguments and shifting metaphors. Two preliminary guidelines are helpful as we forge ahead. First of all, 3:7–18 is an exegetical discussion of Exodus 34, in particular verses 29–35. This is the well-known account of Moses going up to Mt. Sinai to receive a second set of stone tablets from God. After receiving the Law from God, Moses returns to the Israelites; but unbeknownst to himself, as a result of his having seen God his face shines with a glorious countenance so resplendent that no Israelites dare to approach him at first. To make it possible for the Israelites to do so, Moses puts on a veil after he finishes speaking with the people and takes it off only when he goes into the presence of the Lord. As we can see, all the important elements in 2 Cor 3:7–18 come from the Exodus account: the shining face of Moses (verse 7; compare with Exod 34:29–30), the veil (verse 13; Exod 34:33), and Moses taking off the veil before the Lord (verse 16; Exod 34:34). Other references to the stone tablets (3:3) and covenants (3:4–6) can be found in Exod 34:1, 4, 10–28 as well. Paul's discussion, accordingly, follows the Exodus account, devoting verses 7–11 to the exegesis of Exod 34:29–32, and verses 12–18 to Exod 34:33–34.

Secondly, when Paul interprets Moses' ascent to Mt. Sinai to see the Lord face to face as well as the believers' encounter with the Spirit (verses 16–18), he presupposes a common first-century Hellenistic-Jewish tradition that can be called, for lack of a better word, mysticism. In this mystical tradition, the highest form of attainment is a vision of God, an encounter with the divine, which would result in a transformation of the seer. This is exactly how the first-century Jewish commentator Philo of Alexandria interprets the ascent of Moses to Mt. Sinai to face God:

> For we read that by God's command [Moses] ascended an inaccessible and pathless mountain, the highest and most sacred in the region, and remained for the period named, taking nothing that is needed to satisfy the requirements of bare sustenance. Then, after the said forty days had passed, he descended, so that those who saw him were filled with awe and amazement; none of their eyes could even continue to stand the dazzling brightness that flashed from him like the rays of the sun (*Life of Moses* 2:70).

Paul evidently agrees that this is what Moses had achieved. His ascent to Mt. Sinai to receive the Law granted him the extraordinary experience of having seen the Lord, and this encounter resulted in a changed countenance. To Paul, all this is evidence that the Mosaic covenant "came about in splendor" (verse 7). But Paul sets Moses up only to denigrate him, which he does in verses 7–11. Surely the Mosaic covenant was resplendent, evidenced by the glorious splendor on the face of Moses. But if the inferior covenant was characterized by splendor and glory, how much more glorious will the superior covenant be! "If the ministry of death...came in splendor, ...how much more resplendent will the ministry of Spirit be?" (verses 7–8).

To identify the Mosaic covenant as a ministry of death is a rather harsh judgment. To see how Paul reaches this conclusion, we need to look at the larger pattern of antithetical comparisons that begins with the letter-*versus*-Spirit contrast established in verse 6. To list all the terms of comparison found in verses 7–11 in Paul's dichotomous pattern, the following table obtains:

LETTER AND SPIRIT

(verse 6)	Letter Kills	Spirit Gives Life
verses 7–8	Ministry of Death	Ministry of the Spirit
verse 9	Ministry of Condemnation	Ministry of Righteousness
verse 11	That which is abolished	That which abides
(Implied)	Mosaic Covenant	New Covenant

This table functions in a binary fashion, which is to say that each column is exclusive of the other, so that if a term does not belong to one column, it is automatically assigned to its opposite. Given this premise, if the new covenant is so surpassingly superior to the old that the Mosaic covenant pales in comparison, this can only mean that the Mosaic covenant does not belong to the new and is in fact its opposite. If the new covenant is characterized by the Spirit which gives life, so the argument goes, the Mosaic covenant must be characterized by its opposite, death. Therefore, "That which had splendor has become no splendor at all in this regard on account of the surpassing glory" (verse 10), which has come through Christ.

Paul's mode of argumentation in these verses gives us a clue to his opponents' position, against which all of Paul's theological arguments are trained. The *a fortiori* argument of "if . . . , how much more . . . ," which was a well-known Jewish method of interpretation used by Paul on other occasions as well, could make sense only if Paul's readers are convinced, first, that the Mosaic covenant is basically sound; and, second, that the new covenant is superior. The only position to which both these conditions apply would be a view of a new covenant that is inextricably bound up with the written law of Moses. This goes back to our earlier discussion that Paul's debate with his opponents is over *what type* of new covenant Christ represents: Is it one that is based on the Mosaic Law? That would be the position of Paul's opponents. Or is it based on an encounter of the eschatological Spirit? That is what Paul advocates in this passage. Both Paul and his opponents would self-consciously claim their positions as consistent with the eschatological new covenant. The only difference is how this new covenant is characterized: is it by the law of Moses or by a live experience of the Spirit. Herein lies the issue of contention between the two camps.

A new covenant based on the Mosaic Law was not unknown to Paul. He had already encountered it in Galatia, where Jewish-Christian preachers, the so-called Judaizers, came to the church in Paul's absence advocating the need to be faithful to the Mosaic Law. Paul is most likely thinking of this same position when he says that "the letter kills." In contrast to the surpassing glory of the life-giving Spirit that energizes the new covenant, the Law codes can only appear to induce death.

Paul is well aware of the major difference that separates himself from his Hellenistic-Jewish enemies, and that is why he sets out to demonstrate the superiority of the Spirit over the Mosaic Law. He does this by appealing to the experience of the Corinthians — that is, their experience of the Spirit at their conversion. Once they take experience as the primary datum in their reference point, they will see — so goes the argument — that the Mosaic Law belongs to an old covenant that is in the process of fading and that is being abolished. No matter what the law-centered missionaries might claim to the contrary, the surpassing glory of the splendid new covenant has rendered the Mosaic Law obsolete. Those who advocate the Law may not realize it, but the Law is part of the old covenant and therefore should not be revived in the new; those who still do live under the old covenant.

Note, however, that Paul has to make a minor adjustment to the biblical account to make his point. The original Exodus account says that the Israelites "were afraid to come near" Moses because of his face (Exod 34:30); it does not say explicitly that the Israelites were unable to look into Moses' face because of its splendor. In fact, according to Exod 34:33, Moses put on a veil *after* he finished addressing the people, which would imply that he addresses the people with his face shown to them. To this, Paul adds, "the Israelites *could not gaze intently into the face of Moses*" (verse 7). In the passage cited earlier, Philo had said something similar about the effect the face of Moses had on the Israelites: "None of their eyes could even continue to stand the dazzling brightness that flashed from him like the rays of the sun." There is no evidence that Paul ever read Philo, but this shows Paul's exegesis of Exodus was not pursued in a vacuum but was part and parcel of a first-century Jewish exegetical tradition.

Paul lays such emphasis on the people's inability to gaze into Moses' glorious countenance — to the point of repeating it in verse 13 — because the new narrative logic now allows him to focus on the veil placed on the face of Moses. The veil will now become the center of his exegetical attention in the rest of chapter 3 (verses 12-18). In verse 13, Paul first suggests that Moses put his veil on to hide the fading splendor, which for Paul symbolizes the passing of the old covenant (see also verse 7). This fading glory of Moses is not mentioned in the Exodus account, even though nothing in the biblical text, especially Exod 34:33, would contradict that observation. It is, rather, something stipulated by Paul's antithetical contrasts of verses 7–11. Since the new covenant discloses abiding glory, glory that cannot fade, the implication is that the inferior Mosaic covenant must belong to the realm of transitory glory.

But what Paul does next with the veil, in verses 14–15, can only be called an exegetical sleight of hand: he transfers the veil from the face of *Moses* to *the hearts and minds of Paul's fellow Jews!* The result is that "their minds were hardened, for even to this very day *the same veil* remains upon their reading of the old covenant" (verse 14) and that "until today, whenever Moses is read, *a veil* covers their heart" (verse 15). What gives Paul the license to make this transfer?

Paul's method is not as mad as it initially appears. What we need to keep in mind is that the veil stands between Moses and the Israelites and therefore represents a barrier, an obstacle. "Moses" and "Israelites," on the other hand, do double duties in Paul's argument: "Moses" stands for the historical lawgiver as well as for the Jewish Law, the Torah, while "Israelites" represents the biblical Hebrews as well as Paul's Jewish contemporaries. Paul's view of the Bible in this respect was not that different from other Jewish interpreters of the first century; they all saw the text not as a merely historical document but as eternally valid scripture applicable to all contemporary persons and events. Once these elements are in place, the biblical veil standing between Moses and the Israelites (verse 13) is then contemporized to become the modern veil standing between their modern counterparts. In other words, for Paul, the Exodus account really describes how his fellow Jews are reading the Law of Moses without enlightenment or understanding, as if a veil still enshrouded their minds, concealing the real meaning of the text from them.

What Paul means by enlightenment is obviously true knowledge of Christ, and this can come about only by lifting the veil. Jews of Paul's days still read Moses with veiled hearts and minds, according to Paul's argument, because the veil, which is abolished only in Christ, remains unlifted (verse 14). How is it to be lifted? Here in verse 16 Paul performs one last exegetical maneuver, and it again involves a subtle modification of a biblical text, this time Exod 34:34. The best way to visualize Paul's interpretative changes is to view the original text and Paul's version synoptically.

PAUL'S READING OF EXODUS

Exod 34:34	*2 Cor 3:16*
Whenever <u>Moses</u> <u>went</u> <u>in</u> <u>before</u> the Lord <u>to</u> <u>speak</u> <u>with</u> <u>him,</u> <u>he</u> <u>would</u> <u>remove</u> the veil....	Whenever <u>one</u> <u>turns</u> <u>to</u> the Lord, the veil <u>is</u> <u>removed.</u>

Paul's changes in this case do not seem nearly as drastic as before; they at first seem no more than a paraphrase of the original text. But the effects are nothing short of revolutionary. First of all, "Moses" is taken out of the Exodus passage, and "went in before" is changed to the pregnant phrase "turns to." "To turn to" was a technical term for conversion in the early church; Paul uses the verb with that meaning in 1 Thess 1:9; Gal 4:9. The word was also used with this connotation in Acts 9:35; 11:21 and elsewhere in 1 Pet 2:25. Its use here cannot be accidental. Next, Paul excises the phrase "to speak with him" from the text, thus turning a verse about a specific action of Moses into a general statement about an encounter with the Lord. Finally, Paul changes the main verb from an active voice ("he would remove") into a passive voice ("is removed"). The result of these changes is a new text that is no longer about Moses' doffing his own veil when he goes into the Lord's presence but about the believers' having their veil lifted if they abandon their old ways and turn to the Lord. The believers' veil over their hearts and minds will be removed — by "the Lord" — if they turn to him. Just in case there is any doubt about what he intends to say, Paul in verse 17 appends an explanatory note: "The Lord" of Exod 34:34 is to be identified with the very eschatological Spirit that believers experienced in the context of their own conversion.[7] Paul again demonstrates the Bible has contemporary relevance by applying it directly to his peers.

The result of the encounter of the Spirit, with "an unveiled face," is a total transformation of the seer (verse 18). Paul uses a mirror metaphor to speak of the vision, as if one sees one's own reflection in the process. The precise meaning of "mirror" is open to dispute, but it is possible that Paul is alluding again to the Hellenistic-Jewish understanding that a vision of the divine results in the progressive transformation of the seer into the image of the divine. Believers who turn to the Spirit with an unveiled face will ascend the ladder of glory and be transformed in the process, "from one degree of glory to another."

This is in stark contrast to Moses, who had to put on a veil to conceal the splendor that was fading with time (verses 7, 13). If all this is true, then Paul is making a significant claim about the believers' own encounter with the resurrected Lord. Not only could believers experience the very vision of God that Moses had on Mt. Sinai; they in fact could surpass him in acquiring the permanent splendor that endures. Here Paul's polemical edge comes into play again, just as he has done with subtlety in verses 7–11. When Paul unfavorably compares Moses to the extraordinary experiences that his readers all share, he intends it as a snub to those who would elevate the status of Moses and the Law. Since what the Spirit has wrought in the lives and experiences today is far superior to even what Moses received, why then be seduced by an inferior brand of teachings?

There is a related strategy lying behind Paul's rhetorics throughout chapter 3, and that is his ambiguous use of the first person plural "we." It is not always clear whether Paul uses it to refer exclusively to himself and colleagues or inclusively to all his readers as well. In 3:1–3, where Paul distinguishes between "we" and "you," there is no question that "we" refers only to himself. This also seems to continue in verses 4–6 where he broaches the subject of competent ministers for the new covenant. But by the time we come to the climactic section of verses 12–18, "we" becomes far more ambiguous. Verse 12, "With such hope, *we* behave with great boldness," seems to echo verse 4 and anticipates 4:1 later, but the emphatic "we, all of us" of verse 18 is clearly inclusive of all believers as well as himself. What Paul hopes to achieve here is to use himself as a model for direct encounter with the glory of God; this encounter is open to all and is in fact the essence and foundation of the Corinthians' very own experience.

Paul begins chapter 3 by recalling his intimate relationship with the Corinthian congregation, by which he obviously intends to draw the Corinthians closer to himself. But ultimately he wants to convince the Corinthians that they have sufficient resources in themselves, so that they have no need to rely on anyone, least of all outside missionaries. Paul accomplishes both of these goals by holding himself up as a model for their spiritual life. Inviting his congregations to imitate him in all things (see, e.g., 1 Thessalonians) has always been part of Paul's general missionary strategy, but here it serves a different function. He holds his own spiritual life up as a paradigm for the Corinthians, so that his readers can also feel confident that they have acquired the same sufficiency which he has been granted by God (3:12). It is in this interchange between the personal and the congregational, in the paradigmatic concept of the self, that his discourse on "confidence" and "competence" (3:4–6) makes sense. With this he returns to his relationship with the church in Corinth and the question of competency, first raised in verses 14–16, that touches off the exegetical discussion of chapter 3.[8]

Concluding Comments on the Ministry of Glory: 4:1–6

4 [1]Therefore, with this ministry, as we have been given mercy, we do not lose heart, [2]but we renounce the hidden things of shame, not behaving in craftiness or falsifying the word of God, but in openness of truth recommending ourselves to every human conscience before God. [3]If our gospel is also veiled, it is veiled to those who are perishing. [4]The god of this age has blinded the mind of the unbelievers, so that they do not see the light of the gospel of glory of Christ, who is an image of God. [5]For we preach not ourselves but Jesus Christ as Lord and ourselves as your servants on account of Jesus. [6]For the God who said, "Out of darkness a light shines forth," is he who shone forth in our hearts in order to enlighten us with the knowledge of the glory of God in the face of [Jesus] Christ.

When Paul first posed the question, "Who is competent to be God's minister?" in 2:16, his readers had expected, "No one!" Now that Paul has delineated the superiority of the new covenant, the ministry of glory, readers have even more reason to assume a negative answer. But just as before, in 3:4–6, Paul explains how God alone equips authentic ministers for this work, so here, too, he reinforces his reliance on God. "We do not lose heart" of 4:1 parallels, albeit negatively, "we behave with great boldness" of 3:12 and anticipates similar statements in 4:16 and

5:6. The basis for not losing heart, not being discouraged by the crushing responsibilities of the ministry, is that God has shown mercy to Paul.

Just as this passage continues the previous discussion, it also advances it by drawing on what he has said about divine encounter. "We have been given mercy" likely alludes to the encounter of the Spirit with "unveiled face" mentioned in 3:16–18; it is the subsequent transformation that emboldens Paul and his ministry. But "unveiled face" means to Paul more than a metaphor for enlightenment; it is also a symbol of honesty and openness. Unlike Moses who used the veil to conceal the inferiority of his ministry, Paul claims that he has removed his own veil, he renounces all hidden things that are shameful, and behaves in openness (4:2). Nevertheless, Paul does admit that his gospel could appear veiled to some, probably reflecting a mysterious charge leveled against him by his detractors, though it is uncertain what that charge might be. But if his message appears veiled, Paul responds, it is so only because those who cannot comprehend it have been blinded by "the god of this age," Satan himself (4:3–4).

Paul concludes his discussion on the ministry of glory in 4:6 with a reference to God in creation (Gen 1:3):[9] "The God who said, 'Out of darkness a light shines forth,' is he who shone forth in our hearts in order to enlighten us with the knowledge of the glory of God in the face of Christ." It has been suggested that the language of enlightenment here refers to Paul's own conversion experience, but elsewhere when Paul refers to that experience (Gal 1:15–16; 1 Cor 15:8–11), he describes it in terms of revelation not illumination.[10] It is more likely that Paul intends the verse more generally, since it is structured as a contrast to 4:4 as well as a recapitulation of the transformative language of 3:18. Inasmuch as the god of this world has blinded those who are perishing, the God of creation shines a great light on the hearts of those being saved and gives them knowledge about the glory of God. These contrasting responses are precisely what Paul says his message would solicit, and thus we come full circle to the introductory section of 2:14–16.

Ministry of Hardship: 4:7–5:10

4 [7]We have this treasure in clay vessels, so that the surpassing power might be understood as belonging to God and not to us.

⁸In every thing, we are afflicted but not crushed, discouraged but not hopelessly despairing, ⁹persecuted but not forsaken, struck down but not destroyed, ¹⁰always carrying the death of Jesus in our body, so that the life of Jesus might be manifested in our body as well. ¹¹For always we who are living are delivered up to death for Jesus' sake, in order that the life of Jesus might also be manifested in our mortal flesh. ¹²The end result is that death is at work in us, but life in you. ¹³With the same spirit of faith according to what is written, "I believed; therefore I spoke" [Ps 116:10], we too believe; therefore we also speak, ¹⁴knowing that he who raised the Lord Jesus will raise us also with Jesus and present us with you. ¹⁵For all things are done on your behalf, so that grace, abounding through many, may increase thanksgiving for the glory of God.

¹⁶Therefore, we do not lose heart. Even though our outer person is wasting away, our inner person is renewed day by day. ¹⁷For the momentary trifle of our affliction produces in us an eternal weight of glory beyond all measure, ¹⁸for we look not at things that are seen but at what are unseen, because what are seen are temporary, but what are unseen are eternal. 5 ¹For we know that if our earthly tent is destroyed, we have a dwelling from God, an eternal house made without hand in the heavens. ²In this regard, we sigh, yearning to be clothed with our dwelling from heaven; ³if indeed we are clothed, we will not be found naked. ⁴For while we are in this tent we sigh, being weighed down, because we do not want to be unclothed but clothed, so that the mortal might be swallowed up by life. ⁵The God who has worked in us for this very purpose is he who has given us the down payment of the Spirit.

⁶Therefore, being confident always and knowing that while we are at home in the body we are away from the Lord — ⁷for through faith we walk, not through sight — ⁸we are confident and would be more pleased to dwell out of the body and to dwell with the Lord. ⁹Therefore, we also aspire, whether dwelling in or out, to be pleasing to him. ¹⁰For all of us must appear before the judgment seat of Christ, in order that each might receive the reward according to what each has done in the body, whether good or evil.

If Paul had stopped at the end of the last section, he could well have been accused of preaching the very same gospel of power and strength for which he criticizes his opponents. Instead, Paul immediately juxtaposes to the ministry of glory a ministry of hardship. If the ministry of glory is characterized by visions of God and transformed countenance, the ministry of hardship is characterized by affliction, suffering, and despair. In fact, hardship is a more appropriate symbol for the authentic minister, because he or she identifies with and carries Jesus' death at all times. This is why Paul presents himself as a captive prisoner whose life might be sacrificed at any moment (see discussion on 2:14–16). The less adequate the minister is, in and of himself or herself, the better he or she is at demonstrating that the power of the gospel comes from God. All this is already implicit in Paul's presentation of the ministry of glory, for its glory is based on God's authority and power, to which the minister plays but a derivative and secondary role. In this section Paul makes this point explicit, and he does so right from the start.

The opening verse, 4:7, is a summation of the whole section, and the rest is in many respects an expansive footnote to it. It begins abruptly, "We have this treasure in clay vessels, so that the surpassing power might be understood as belonging to God and to us." Many have speculated endlessly on the contents of the treasure, but that misses Paul's main point here which is the worthlessness of clay. Unlike jars made of metal which could be melded into new implements even when broken, clay vessels, once cracked or broken, have to be discarded. Paul uses the stark contrast between precious treasure and ignoble clay, therefore, to demonstrate God's pure power that is not mixed with human ability. If by "treasure" Paul means the preaching of the gospel of glory — which seems a reasonable inference from the exegetical discussion of chapter 3 — then with a new metaphor of "clay vessels" he amplifies his earlier idea that inadequate human agency paradoxically accentuates the incomparable power of God in spreading the gospel. His discussion of the hardship he experienced in his apostolate and, more importantly, God's role in preventing difficult situations from becoming desperate in the next two verses would bear this interpretation out.

The catalogue of hardships is a common feature in Paul's letters. We have a flavor of it already in 1:3–11, and we will meet it again later in 6:4–10; 11:23–27; 12:10.[11] But what makes the catalogue of 4:8–9 different is that it is formulated in four antithetical pairs: afflicted but not crushed, discouraged but not hopelessly despairing, persecuted but not forsaken, struck down but not destroyed. The first terms of the comparisons describe the adversities Paul must endure in the course of preaching the gospel; the second describe the results of reliance on God's power. In all cases, what at first appears bleak never becomes hopeless, for the power of God triumphs at the end.

In the history of ideas, the catalogue of hardships was hardly a Pauline invention: Stoic philosophers had long used it to demonstrate the ability of a superior person to rise above adversities and difficult circumstances. For the Stoics, a superior person is one who can marshal internal psychic resources and train the inner disposition, so that he or she can become indifferent to all adversities under whatever circumstance. Paul, however, is advocating precisely the opposite. The source for overcoming adversity comes not from one's inner self; on the contrary the onslaught of adversities could overwhelm a person and can easily show up the person's inability to overcome it. There are no inner resources to which anyone could appeal, which is why one's eventual survival of such adversities can be attributed only to the surpassing power of God. The catalogue of hardships, therefore, documents not the apostle's prowess but his inability to overcome adversity by himself.

That God would inspire unworthy people is nothing new, nor is it particularly Christian; Plato and many other philosophers have espoused similar ideas down through the ages. What makes Paul's statement unique, though, is the basic fundamental unity between Christ and believers that underlies his whole discussion of hardship. Not in spite of but in the midst of affliction, Paul says that he "always [carries] the death of Jesus in the body" and that "always we who are living are delivered up to death for Jesus' sake" (4:10a, 11a). This verse is syntactically linked to the adversities of verses 8–9 but introduces a new thought. The basis on which Paul has the confidence that God's power will always be manifested in his adversities is the apostle's daily identification with Christ's suffering and death. Paul understood his own sufferings not as an imitation of Christ nor as sufferings in the service of Jesus, as in the case of the second-century martyr bishop Ignatius of Antioch. Instead, he is profoundly convinced that the sufferings and death of Christ are somehow replicated in his own bodily afflictions. It is this deep identification with Christ's death that gives Paul the firm hope that "the life of Jesus might be manifested in our body as well" and that "the life of Jesus might also be manifested in our mortal flesh" (4:10b, 11b).

Identifying with the death of Jesus is of course a signature theme in Paul's theology. In 1:5, where Paul says "the sufferings of Christ overflow into us," we had occasion to see how he fits this into his self-understanding of his apostolic mission. But elsewhere he generalizes this notion of identification into a characteristic trait of Christian life. In Gal 2:19–20, he speaks autobiographically but intends it to be broadly applied to all believers: "I have been crucified with Christ: it is no longer I who live but Christ who lives in me." Later in Romans 6 where he elaborates on the significance of baptism for all believers, he understands it as an identification with Christ's death: "Therefore, we have been buried with him through baptism unto death, so that just as Christ was raised from the dead through the glory of the father, thus also we ourselves will walk in newness of life. For if we have become, and continue to be, united in a death like his, then we will certainly be united in a resurrection like his" (6:4–5; see also verses 3, 8). In 2 Cor 5:14–15 he will reiterate this point in order to prepare his readers for the ministry of reconciliation. For now, Paul just wants to emphasize the common theological basis uniting all believers, which is the shared confidence that identification with Christ's death will lead to life. This is so because of the resurrection of Christ. Just as God raised Christ from the dead, God will "raise us also with Jesus and present us together with you" (4:14).

In saying that "the life of Jesus will be manifested in our mortal flesh" (verse 11), however, Paul does not say that God will deliver Christians from bodily harm or danger. Paul is advancing no magical formula for avoiding life's miseries; it is only that in the continual death the believer experiences every day, God will make the life of Jesus palpably and progressively visible in the midst of calamities. It is as if the believer at once led two separate lives, one inner and one outer. The outer life experiences the forces of mortality and comes under the sway of corruption, degeneration, decay, and death; it "wastes away" (4:16) until it is utterly "destroyed" (5:1). But the inner life belongs to the realm of regeneration, replenishment, restoration, and resurrection; "it is renewed day by day" (4:16), in the same way that the believer who encounters the Spirit with unveiled faces is transformed from one degree of glory to another (3:18). Paul uses the same terminology in Rom 7:22–23, where "inner man" is a synonym for "mind," and later on in the same letter he identifies the mind as that which is continually being renewed and transformed by the Spirit (Rom 12:2).

Paul's language of inner *versus* outer at first sight reminds us of such dualism as body *versus* spirit current in the Hellenistic thought world. Paul's complex of dualistic contrasts could further reinforce this suspicion: besides the contrast between the "outer person" and "inner person" (4:16), there is the "seen" *versus* "unseen" (4:18), "earthly tent" *versus* "heavenly dwelling" (5:1-2, 4), naked *versus* clothed (5:3-4), mortal *versus* death (5:4). We ought not push the ontological distinction between the inner and outer persons too much, however, since Paul does not make extensive use of this terminology. He uses these terms metaphorically to describe the process of renewal: the contrast between the "outer" and "inner" is a contrast between the state of hardships and the overcoming of them.

Nevertheless Paul does presuppose some kind of dualism, but it is one that is qualified and conditioned by time, or more properly by the end of time, the *eschaton*. To the kind of static, timeless dualism that we have come to expect from Hellenism, Paul makes a telling modification: "What are seen are *temporary*, but what are unseen are *eternal*" (4:18). The outer person, the earthly tent, even death, will all be replaced by the inner person, our heavenly abode, and finally eternal life. This is why Paul is able to describe the affliction he experiences in his ministry a "momentary trifle" that will produce "an eternal weight of glory beyond all measure" (4:17). Even when he presents the body as a barrier to a more perfect participation in Christ — so much so that "while we are in this tent we sigh under a burden, because we do not want to be unclothed but clothed" (5:4) and "while we are at home in the body we are away from the Lord" (5:6), a sentiment he also expresses in Phil 1:21-23 — he does so within the context of the last day. In the believers' yearning to be clothed with the heavenly dwelling, God has given them the Spirit as a "down payment" for the full payment as a guarantee that perfection will be realized in the final consummation. Paul makes the same point about the Corinthians' present experience of the Spirit, "The God who establishes us with you in Christ and anointed us, is also he who has stamped us with his seal and given the Spirit in our hearts as *down payment*" (2 Cor 1:21-22).

Finally, in the last judgment, each will be rewarded or punished according to what each has done "in the body" (5:10). Far from thinking that the body is inherently evil, Paul presents it with all its limitations and restrictions, as the only avenue for ethical behaviors, "whether good or evil," behaviors that will be evaluated before the "judgment seat of Christ" at the end. Paul actively looks forward to the return of Christ, the parousia, at which point general resurrection will take place, judgment will take place, and the faithful will be rewarded according to their ethical behaviors.[12] But note that Paul is not advocating a position of earning rewards with his affliction, as if suffering could become ground for a perverse kind of boasting. Rather, Paul simply looks forward to the end time when he will be vindicated. What we have in Paul is an eschatological rather than an ontological dualism.

It is his utter certainty that God will keep the promise in the end times that proves to be the ground for Paul's confidence. As we have seen already, Paul repeatedly declares his confidence in his ministry (see, e.g., 3:4, 12; 4:1). Even in the face of hardship and despair and the seeming inevitability of one's mortality, Paul steadfastly asserts that he does not lose heart (4:16; 5:6, 8). The basis for such confidence is his conviction that God will establish right judgment in the final day, because of what is, to Paul, the objective reality of the resurrection of Christ.

Throughout his discussion of the ministry of hardship, Paul emphasizes the common bond he has with the Corinthians in suffering and in shared life. Just as he could suggest in 1:7 that the Corinthians somehow share his sufferings,[13] here in 4:12, he makes a transfer from his suffering and death to the congregation's life: "Death is at work *in us*, but life *in you*." In affliction and in death, Paul tells them, he toils for the preaching of the gospel, so that they could have the benefit of life in Christ. Citing Ps 116:10, "I believed; therefore I spoke," Paul reminds the Corinthians of the sacrifice he and fellow-missionaries have made in order to preach the gospel to them. "All things are done on your behalf, so that grace, abounding through many, may increase thanksgiving for the glory of God" (4:15). All this anticipates his final move when he turns his attention to the burning problem that prompted his extensive discourse on the true nature of ministry in the first place, to salvage his relationship with his Corinthian converts. He does this in the third movement of his presentation, the ministry of reconciliation.

Ministry of Reconciliation:
5:11–21

[11]Knowing, therefore, the fear of the Lord, we persuade people, but we have been made known to God. I hope to be made known to your consciences as well. [12]We do not again recommend ourselves to you but give you an opportunity of boasting on our behalf, in order that you may have something to say to those who boast in appearance and not in heart. [13]For if we are in ecstasy, it is for God; if we are sober-minded, it is for you.

[14]For the love of Christ holds us together. Our judgment is this, that one died for all; therefore, all died [15]and he died for all, in order that those who live might live no longer for themselves but for him who died and was raised up for them.

[16]Thus, from now on we know no one according to the flesh; though we knew Christ according to the flesh, now we no longer know him this way. [17]Thus, if anyone is in Christ, there is a new creation. The old things have passed; behold, new things have come to be. [18]All things come from God who has reconciled us to himself through Christ and who has given us the ministry of reconciliation. [19]As it is said, "God was, in Christ, reconciling the world to himself, not reckoning their trespasses against them," and entrusting to us the word of reconciliation. [20]On behalf of Christ, therefore, we are commissioned, while God appeals through us. We beseech you on behalf of Christ: Be reconciled to God! [21]On our behalf he made him sin who knew no sin, in order that by him we might become the righteousness of God through him.

As we have seen in our discussion of 2:17–3:3, lurking in the background of Paul's prose is a group of itinerant missionaries to whom Paul is being unfavorably compared. Judging from Paul's reactions — moderate here but much more virulent elsewhere (notably chapters 10–13) — problems occasioned by their arrival are most likely the prime motivation for writing the current letter. But if that is the case, that is not how Paul presents it to his readers. Though Paul here and there would drop references to these outsider preachers, he consistently constructs the problem, at least rhetorically, as the deteriorating relationship between him and the Corinthians. It is a problem that threatens to break apart the community and separate Paul from them, one which the congregation must try to solve by turning away from the outsiders' seductive overtures and becoming reconciled with Paul.

The solution to this problem, Paul suggests to his readers, begins with recognizing the true character of the ministry ordained by God. Authentic ministry is characterized not by an extravagant display of the minister's power and might, but by the glory of God who is the prime cause of all spiritual competence. The human agents in this ministry of glory are likened to ignoble earthenware, fragile and unworthy, beset with mortal frailty; nevertheless, they have confidence and speak with boldness in spite of momentary afflictions, only because the God who raised Christ from the dead will surely endow them with an eternal weight of glory at the parousia. God's cosmic plan underlies everything the true minister does, and that plan is God's reconciling the world to God's self. Paul accordingly issues a challenge to the wayward Corinthians: "Will you be a part of this divine plan and are you ready to be reconciled to God? And if you are, will you accord God's ministers their rightful place in this new economy and will you be reconciled to them?"

Paul begins by addressing the Corinthians directly in a way that he has not done since the beginning of his discourse on authentic ministry, as we can readily see from the language of the opening paragraph (5:11-13). "We do not again recommend ourselves" (5:12) recalls the charge that Paul does not carry with him letters of recommendation from reputed authorities the way his opponents, the itinerant preachers, do, a charge to which he responded back in 3:1-3. "Those who boast in appearance and not in heart" (5:12) must likewise refer to the same group to whom Paul derisively refers as "peddlers of God's word" (2:17). Boasting in their appearance but not in their heart is probably Paul's way of saying they revel in their showy strengths but are otherwise superficial charlatans.

To these by-now-familiar traits of the opponents, Paul adds another one: "For if we are in ecstasy, it is for God; if we are sober-minded, it is for you" (5:13). "Ecstasy" (NRSV, "beside ourselves") refers to the common first-century phenomenon of divinely inspired enthusiasm resulting in such mantic behaviors as glossolalia (that is, speaking in tongues), visions, trances, and out-of-body journeys. Paul was no stranger to these religious experiences. In 1 Corinthians 14, Paul admits to the positive values of speaking in tongues which he calls speaking the "mysteries of the Spirit" (verse 2). He wishes that "all would speak in tongues" (verse 5) but explains that ecstatic speech requires interpretation (12:10). Later in 2 Cor 12:1-4, Paul relates an extraordinary experience of his being caught up in the third heaven; this happened "whether in the body I do not know, whether out of the body I do not know, God knows" (verse 2 and repeated in verse 3). But Paul's attitude towards ecstasy has been consistent all along: Since glossolalia addresses one's speech only to God (1 Cor 14:2) and not to one's fellow-worshippers, without interpretation it will benefit no one but the speaker (1 Cor 14:4-5). Paul himself speaks in tongues in abundance (1 Cor 14:18), but he immediately qualifies it by saying, "in church I would rather speak five words with my mind, in order to instruct others also, than ten thousand words in a tongue" (1 Cor 14:19). With regard to his journey to the third heaven, he is goaded into sharing it — so he claims — because his opponents continually boast of such experiences (2 Cor 12:1, 11). Even so, he immediately deconstructs that gaudy experience by telling his readers how God slowed him down with weaknesses (12:5-10). Paul tells his detractors that while he has an ample storehouse of such ecstatic experiences to persuade the doubters, he refrains by choice from boasting of them, for only a sober-minded ministry could ultimately benefit the life of the congregation.

But Paul's real audience in this dialogue is not his opponents but the Corinthians whom he addresses directly throughout this passage. Paul accomplishes this rhetorically by switching back and forth between what he and his fellow-workers have done in the "we"-passages and what the Corinthians must do in response in the "you"-passages. "*We* persuade people and *we* have been made known to God"; therefore, "I hope to be made known to *your consciences* as well" (5:11). "*We* do not again recommend *ourselves*," so that "*you* [would have] an opportunity [to boast] on our behalf, . . . to say to those who boast in their external appearance" (5:12). One aim of this is obviously to remind the Corinthians of their solidarity with Paul and convince them that what he has done is for their benefit. But this piece of rhetoric also forces the Corinthians to choose between Paul and his opponents, between heeding seriously what Paul has done and discrediting him entirely. What they cannot do is ignore him in silence. The onus is now on the Corinthians.

In the next verses, as he has done in 4:10-11, Paul again appeals to the believers' identification with the death of Christ,

"One died for all; therefore, all died and he died for all, in order that those who live might live no longer for themselves but for him who died and was raised up for them" (5:14–15). "All" here appears to be generally inclusive, but because Paul has just established the Corinthians as the primary focus of his rhetorical attention, it applies specifically to them even though they are not explicitly named. By the same token, the use of the first person plural throughout this passage refers not just to Paul and his coworkers but especially to the Corinthians as a community. Paul does this in order to compel the Corinthians to face up to the consequences of what they already believe in.

"One died for all" (verse 14b) is most likely a formula in the apostolic church well known to the whole congregation, which is why Paul does not take time to demonstrate its validity. But Paul goes on to say that this means all believers, specifically the Corinthians, are now living in a radically new existence as a result of their identification with the Christ's death. The mortal body to which everyone is subjected renders "all" as good as dead. What life that is evident in the believers is therefore not a result of any self-regeneration or self-renewal but a result of Christ's having died for all. The believers' life is freely granted to them, and they owe it to the death and resurrection of Christ who enlivens all who by rights should be dead. If that is the case, the logical conclusion is that they now must dedicate their existence to Christ who made this transformation possible in the first place.

Not only that, this new existence also carries with it new knowledge and a new perspective. Inasmuch as life is marked off from decay and death, so the new existence must be similarly marked off from the old existence, and life in Christ should be radically distinguished from the realm of the flesh. This is why Paul could proclaim in the next verse, "From now on, we know no one according to the flesh" (verse 16a). The phrase, "Though we knew Christ according to the flesh, now we no longer know him this way" (verse 16b), has been open to a variety of interpretations. They range from a distinction between knowing the historical Jesus and the Christ of faith,[14] to a distinction between a political interpretation of Jesus' Messiahship ("according to the flesh") and a glorified and exalted one.[15] But this might be reading too much into the text. It seems clear that here Paul is simply drawing out the implications of the believers' new existence, and the two contrasting attitudes towards Christ, acceptance or rejection are precisely what characterize the old and new existence. In fact, whether one accepts Christ determines whether one has been transferred from the old realm to the new.

But acceptance of Christ and the resultant new knowledge and perspective are not simply a state of mind, so far as Paul is concerned. Unlike the Stoic philosophers, Paul does not deal with existence merely by adjusting his attitude or disposition towards the unchangeable events of the world. Transfer to the new realm of Christ — or using Paul's favorite expression, to be "in Christ" — is an objective event accompanied by the palpable presence of the Spirit and the concrete manifestation of its power. According to Paul's apocalyptic theology, Christ's death and resurrection have set in motion a series of cosmic events that will lead to the ultimate restoration of the brokenness of the world, and the believers' new existence in Christ is only an instance of the much larger complex of changes. That is why the apostle could boldly proclaim, "If anyone is in Christ, there is a new creation" (5:17a). Being in Christ is not only the consequence of God's cosmic plan; it is also the documentation for the onset of the new creation.

It would be a mistake to understand "new creation" in an individualistic sense, as interpreters for generations have done when they translated the verse as, "If anyone is in Christ, *he is* a new creation."[16] The context speaks against such a translation, since Paul goes on to bring out the cosmic dimension of this verse: "*Old things* have passed. . . . *All things* come from God" (verses 17–18) and "God was in Christ reconciling the *world* to himself" (verse 19). Furthermore, to call an individual a "new creation" would have been foreign to the type of apocalyptic Jewish thinking from which Paul draws his imagery. According to one Jewish apocalyptic tradition, the fall of the first humans irrevocably fractured the original creation, so much so that men and women have come to be permanently alienated from the creator God. Death was let loose in the world and continues to reign it, and the whole created order has been plagued by degeneration and decay ever since. The whole creation yearns to be freed from this bondage, as Paul states so eloquently in Rom 8:19–22. The world has been broken, and we can only hope for its eventual repair; this eager expectation is what stands behind the traditional Hebrew expression, *tikkun ha-olam*, "restoration of the whole world."

Paul's understanding of "new creation" reflects this Jewish

tradition and even goes beyond it. The new creation expresses a hope for the fulfillment that, through Christ, God has already set in motion the cosmic reversal of the primordial fall, that the evil let loose in the world as a result of the fall is beginning to be reined in, that the age-old fissures in the old creation are being mended, that death is being defeated and overturned, and that God has already started the long-awaited process of reconciling the hitherto hostile world to God's own self (5:18–19). But "old things have passed; behold, new things have come to be" (5:17b) also goes beyond the traditional idea of returning the world to its pre-fall state. "New things have come to be" refers to an entirely new creation from the ground up. It is not simply the mending of old problems but the creation of a wholly new existence, a new start, a new situation. And just as in the old creation, God takes sole initiative for the new.[17]

Paul expresses this radical newness in yet another way — by means of modifying and going beyond a preexisting creedal formula on reconciliation. Scholars generally recognize that the words, "God was in Christ reconciling the world to himself, but reckoning their trespasses against them" (verse 19), came from an early Christian creed most likely not formulated by Paul himself, but cited by him to make a point. The use of an introductory formula, "As it is said," and the presence of vocabulary uncharacteristic of Paul ("trespasses" in the plural, whereas Paul always uses the singular) all point to its pre-Pauline origins. The idea of God reconciling the world to God's self represents a departure from the prevailing understanding of reconciliation in Hellenistic Judaism. There the standard interpretation was that the fall and the subsequent human sin had so angered God that God must be appeased. The human sinners must therefore take steps to reconcile themselves to God and to propitiate God's anger. Against this background, the Christian creedal formula reversed the roles and understood God to be initiating this cosmic reconciliation. Furthermore, the Christian formula suggests that God effected reconciliation by "not reckoning [humanity's] trespasses against them," thereby canceling the debts of moral depravity humanity has piled up in God's ledger. The logic was probably that since humanity owes its debt to God, only God has the proper authority to effect and to enforce the cancellation. All this paved the way for cosmic reconciliation of humanity to God.

Paul obviously agrees with the theology behind this creedal

formula, or else he would not have cited it here. The cosmic dimension of reconciliation expressed in the creed readily echoes and supports what he wants to focus on: namely, the new creation. But that does not stop him from adapting it to his purpose. The most important change is the role Christ plays in the cosmic reconciliation. The early Christian creed leaves Christ's role rather vague in its formulation: "God was, in Christ, ... " Whatever the phrase might have meant originally, it says nothing about the nature of Christ's agency in the cosmic drama. Paul clarifies it by making Christ's role explicit in verse 18: "All things come from God who has reconciled us to himself *through Christ.*" Recalling his earlier discussion that Christ had died for all (5:14–15), Paul reformulates the role of Christ as effecting the cancellation of the sinners' debts *by means of* his dying on their behalf. This is probably what Paul means by the phrase "through Christ."

Moreover, Christ's death is understood to be an expression of "the love of Christ [that] holds us together" (5:14). It is the love of Christ that motivated him to give up his life for all. And it is love that motivated Christ to submit himself "who knew no sin" to be made sin "on our behalf, in order that we ourselves might become the righteousness of God in him" (5:21). What makes Paul's interpretation of the new creation so radically different from all previous interpretations of it, be they early Christian or traditional Jewish, is that God pursues the reconciliation of humanity to God's self in the context of a new creation. And this new creation is founded, not on the solemnity of justice or righteousness, but on the power of love. This new creation, this new existence, this new life — all to be sharply distinguished from the realm of the flesh — is strictly identified with and characterized by love. In most dogmatic formulations, reconciliation and justification are, of course, not strictly identical. It has been thought that justification entails a right relation with God, while reconciliation means the overcoming of conflicts and estrangement. But here in 2 Corinthians 5, Paul juxtaposes these two concepts together. Justification (literally, "become righteousness") is the means by which sins are taken away (verse 21). But since sin is that which caused humanity to be estranged from God at the dawn of time, when the old creation was fundamentally and irrevocably tainted and broken, a removal of sin is precisely what is needed to make creation whole again. The outcome of the atoning death of Christ, in the final analysis, is reconciliation, the condition that singularly marks the new creation. The world now can be at peace with God again.

It is in the context of the new creation based on love that Paul could claim to be a minister of reconciliation. God appointed Paul to the ministry of reconciliation (5:18), establishing in and through him the word of reconciliation (verse 19). In both verses, God takes the initiative and Christ acts out of love as the agent through whom reconciliation would take effect, and Paul plays a secondary, derivative role. Even in the direct appeal to the Corinthians in verse 20, it is God who makes the appeal to the world "through us," as Paul is appointed ambassador of reconciliation. Then and only then is it legitimate for Paul to beseech the Corinthians, "Be reconciled to God!" (verse 20), but even here Paul does so only "on behalf of Christ."

In making such an intimate connection between *God's* appeal to the world and his own appointment to carry out that ministry for the sake of Christ, Paul must also have in mind his tortured relationship with the Corinthian congregation. The factionalism and fractiousness within the church could not but be seen as a microcosmic representation of humanity's enmity with God now being played out on the Corinthian stage. By hammering out the message of a love-based reconciliation, therefore, Paul claims that, not only is his message *about* reconciliation, but his ministry itself is also part and parcel of achieving this reconciliation. Paul's ministry is not just an insignificant footnote to God's primary creative act of reconciliation but is in truth a constitutive part of it.

Paul's appeal to the Corinthians that started in 5:11–13 thus comes full circle. On the basis of a theological reconception that his ministry is based on reconciliation, a radically new understanding of existence that is based on love, Paul concludes his argument by appealing to the Corinthians directly, "Be reconciled to God!" (verse 20). But the unmistakable implication is, "Be reconciled to each other as well as to me!" If God through Christ has already reconciled all things to God's self and if the new creation is already in train, the local problems in the Corinthian congregation must needs be resolved in like manner. With these words, Paul's elaboration on the authentic character of ministry, the ministry of glory, hardship, and reconciliation, comes to a close. What remains is a personal appeal to the Corinthians.

Paul's Final Appeal to the Corinthians:
6:1–13; 7:2–4

6 **1**While we are working together, we also appeal to you not
to receive the grace of God in vain. **2**For it says, "In acceptable
season I listened to you, and in day of salvation I gave you
succor" [Isa 49:8]. Look! Now is the acceptable season, now
is the day of salvation. **3**We give offense to no one, so that
the ministry might not be faulted. **4**Instead, we as servants of
God recommend ourselves in everything: in great endurance,
in afflictions, wants, dire straits, **5**beatings, imprisonments, riots,
labor, sleeplessness, hunger; **6**in purity, knowledge, patience,
kindness, the Holy Spirit, sincere love, **7**word of truth, the
power of God; through the weapons of righteousness on our
right and left hands, **8**glory and dishonor, slander and praise;
we are thought of as lying and yet we are true, **9**as unknown
and yet we are fully known, as dying and yet, behold, we live,
as punished and yet we are not killed, **10**as sorrowing but we
are always joyful, as poor but we abound in great riches, as
having nothing and yet we possess all things.

11Our mouth is open for you, Corinthians, our heart is wide
open. **12**You are not restricted by us but you are restricted in
your affections. **13**In return, open wide your heart — I say as if
to children — and you **7** **2**make room for us. We have wronged
no one, ruined no one, and taken advantage of no one. **3**I do
not say this to condemn you, for I have said before that you
are in our hearts, to die together and to live together. **4**I have
great confidence towards you, and I have great pride for you.
I am filled with consolation and I overflow with joy in all our
affliction.

A word about the current paragraph division. As in the case of
Paul's travelogue which is broken up after 2:13 and resumed
much later in 7:5 (see chapter 3 for details), the present passage
is another example of contextual dislocation. Right after 6:13,
in the midst of his urging the Corinthians "to open wide" their
hearts to him, Paul's appeal is interrupted — in mid-sentence —
by a completely unrelated passage on yoking with unbelievers (6:14–7:1) and is not resumed until 7:2. 7:2–4 is obviously
a continuation of the earlier discussion, since it begins without warning and without conjunction to the preceding passage:
"Make room for us," a reference to 6:13. The Greek word for

"make room," *chōrein,* is chosen with care as the opposite of its cognate, *stenochōrein,* "to confine," in 6:12. For these reasons, we will treat 6:1–13 and 7:2–4 as a coherent whole and discuss 6:14–7:1 as a parenthetical passage in the next section. We cannot be certain what might have caused the dislocation, but it is possible that 6:14–7:1 was originally a marginal gloss that was inadvertently incorporated into the main text by a later copyist.

This section adds little new material to what Paul has already fully developed in the preceding chapters; every statement and every concept echoes something that has already been explored before. This is because the section is intended as a recapitulation of the whole letter of reconciliation, reiterating major themes introduced earlier and giving Paul one final chance to appeal to the Corinthians' senses. Paul begins by reissuing his urgent appeal: "While we are working together, we also appeal to you not to receive the grace of God in vain" (6:1). The question, With whom is Paul working, seems puzzling at first until we realize the whole verse is a structural parallel to 5:20a, "On behalf of Christ, therefore, we are commissioned, while God appeals through us." What is different between them is that in 5:20a, God does the appealing, not Paul. The difference is really not so great as one might think. While Paul would never arrogate to himself the prerogatives of God, we saw earlier that he is so closely identified with God's ministry of reconciliation that he could passionately entreat the Corinthians, perhaps for God but certainly on behalf of Christ — "Be reconciled to God!" (5:20b). Likewise here, his appeal to the Corinthians is equally urgent and insistent: citing Isa 49:8, he speaks authoritatively, "Look! Now is the acceptable season, now is the day of salvation" (6:2). Paul could easily think of himself as a co-worker with God.

The authoritative voice quickly disappears, however, as Paul turns to answer several mistaken perceptions about him. He first defends himself against the charge of his possibly having offended his hearers by his message (6:3). He does not elaborate on this, for he must have felt that his message of reconciliation speaks for itself. Then he returns to the issue of recommendation again, a point to which he has made references in 3:1–3; 4:2; 5:12. Here as before, he recommends himself to the Corinthians in complete openness, "in everything" (6:4a). That is to say, the Corinthians should be well aware of Paul's behavior among them, and their conscience (4:2; 5:12) should be able to attest to Paul's innocence. They, not some distant authorities, are the best judge of whether Paul's ministry is an authentic one. At this point, as if to recapitulate his personal qualifications one more time, Paul adduces an extensive list of attributes that could well be called "an apostolic catalogue." We have already encountered a catalogue of hardships in 4:8–9, but the catalogue here is broader: it includes not merely hardship but also experiences as well as virtues. In all we can distinguish in form and content four categories:

1. *Hardships:* "In afflictions, wants, dire straits, beatings, imprisonments, riots, labor, sleeplessness, hunger" (verses 4b–5);

2. *Virtues:* "In purity, knowledge, patience, kindness, the Holy Spirit, sincere love, word of truth, the power of God" (verses 6–7a);

3. *Experiences:* "Through the weapons of righteousness on our right hand and left hand, glory and dishonor, slander and praise" (verses 7b–8a); and

4. *Paradoxes:* "We are thought of as lying and yet we are true, as unknown and yet we are fully known, as dying and yet, behold, we live, as punished and yet we are not killed, as sorrowing but we are always joyful, as poor but we abound in great riches, as having nothing and yet we own all things" (verses 8b–10).

The listing of hardships is almost a commonplace in Paul's apostolic defense. Of the terms listed in the first category, almost all can be found elsewhere in Paul's letters. There is no compelling reason to doubt that Paul has experienced all these afflictions, even if we cannot always document them from extant sources. The purpose of the hardship catalogue, as we discussed earlier, is to demonstrate apostolic sincerity, and it is based on the apostle's profound identification with Christ's sufferings and death. The next list, that of virtues, includes traits not all limited to the apostles. In Gal 5:22, for example, Paul lists love as the first fruit of the Holy Spirit, which encompasses also patience and kindness. But the last, "power of God," is perhaps a fitting summary of virtues proper to the apostolic ministry.

The third category probably delineates the extremes that Paul has experienced in his ministry. "Glory and slander, slander and praise" perhaps broadly describes how Paul has been received by hearers of his message. In Galatians, he has been hailed as "an angel of God" (Gal 4:14), but in the same church he also sustained slanders of the sort that roused him to take up his rhetorical arms for self-defense. No doubt his choice of words in verses 7b–8a is also motivated by the ups and downs in the Corinthian church. We will have an occasion to witness an exasperated Paul fending off critical comments about his abilities and the veracity of his words in chapters 10–13. At the same time, Paul can also lavish on the Corinthians glowing terms of endearment (see 7:16; 9:1–2). But no matter what the circumstances are, Paul assures his readers that he is ready to fight the necessary battles. "Weapons of righteousness" refers to the tools with which God has equipped Paul to fight for the ultimate justification of humanity: that is, the preaching of the gospel. The violence imagery is part of the political and military conception of the kingdom of God which has to be defended or expanded by waging wars and by pressing into service warriors like Paul. "Right hand and left hand" could simply suggest that Paul is fully equipped, but in more precise usage it indicates the use of his weapons for both offense and defense.

After laying out his apostolic credentials, Paul brings his enumeration of apostolic attributes to a climax with a final set of contrasts and paradoxes. It has finally become clear why Paul has constructed this elaborate *curriculum vitae*, for this is where he deals with some of specific charges against him. In all, Paul lists seven contrasting pairs in this category. In each of the seven contrasts, the first term describes a mistaken evaluation of the apostle and the second term points to his vindication. With respect to the first pair, lying but found to be true, Paul has been perceived as lying and dishonest most likely in connection with the collection (see 12:16–18), but Paul says he could appeal to the people's conscience which will prove that he is telling the truth (4:2; 5:11). As for unknown and known, Paul says in 1 Cor 4:13 that he has become the refuse of the world, having turned away from its allures of fortune and fame, but according to 5:11 he has become fully known to God and fully known to the Corinthians.

The third pair, dying and life, might as well be an epitome of the entire section going back to 2:14 but especially his discussion on the ministry of hardship in 4:7–5:10. Paul understands himself as a captive slave being led to his execution (2:14–16); in his daily toil for the gospel he suffers afflictions and carries the death of Jesus daily (4:10–11a). But all this is but prelude to the ultimate glory that is already being manifested, since the daily dying of Paul paradoxically makes the life of Jesus more and more visible through his mortal body (4:11b). Paul's point about life, here as before, is not that God has delivered him from death but rather that the message of God's ministry of reconciliation and the Christ's love as manifested by his death on our behalf is proclaimed through Paul's suffering. To reinforce this notion, Paul adds a fourth pair, punished and not killed, which is closely aligned in meaning to the previous one, and a fifth, sorrowing and joyful, which probably describes Paul's general tendency of finding joy in spite of sorrow.

The last two pairs mean much the same thing. Paul and his fellow missionaries cannot be considered to have had many worldly possessions, but they have riches in the gospel. But it is possible that Paul is thinking of his refusal to accept financial support from the Corinthian congregation, a sore point in his relationship with the church (see 1 Cor 9:1–18). He alluded to this already in 2:17, when he called those who receiving support from the church "peddlers of God's word." And he will again deal with the same issue in 11:7–11. Paul contends that his self-imposed poverty is done all for the sake of the gospel, and this is the basis for riches untold.

Nevertheless, even if Paul in these verses has in mind the specific charges against him, he answers them only obliquely. He raises no controversial statements in defense of himself, nor does he accuse the Corinthians directly, but simply includes his answers to these charges as part of an extensive list of apostolic attributes. His tone, in line with the message he just concluded in 5:21, is largely conciliatory, warm, and affectionate. He continues this tone in his final paragraph, 6:11–13; 7:2–4, where he addresses the Corinthians directly but in a friendly way. He refers to them as "children" (6:13), and he declares that "our mouth is open for you" (6:11), which is a Semitic expression for speaking candidly and trustingly, a sentiment amplified by his next declaration, "Our heart is wide open," indicating he is ready to receive the Corinthians into its expanse. This is an appeal to the Corinthians, inviting them not to restrict themselves in showing their affections for Paul and his associates (6:12). "Restricting" is intended here as an antonym to "open" and "wide"; Paul's use here paves the way for him to ask the Corinthians to widen their heart for Paul (6:13; 7:2).

Even in the midst of overflowing good will, Paul makes one last protestation of innocence, "We have wronged no one, ruined no one, and taken advantage of no one" (7:2). Paul uses the same verb, "to take advantage of," in 12:17–18, in the context of defending charges that he had manipulated the collection for Jerusalem for personal gain, and he is likely alluding to the same issue here. Nonetheless, he immediately softens the blow by saying that he is not condemning the Corinthians (7:3a). In fact he cites a well-known first-century declaration of friendship, "to live together and to die together." Paul reverses the order of this saying to "to die... to live" (7:3b), no doubt influenced by his Christian understanding of identifying with the linked death and life of Christ. For it is on that basis that Paul could say that the Corinthians somehow participated in Paul's sufferings (1:4–7). And it is on the same basis that Paul could tell his Corinthian readers that he is given up to death for the sake of Jesus, so that "death is at work in us, but life in you" (4:12; see also 4:15).

To end his appeal, Paul expresses his positive feelings towards the Corinthians in a quadruple affirmation: Great confidence, great boast, consolation, and abounding in joy (7:4). All four are expressed in the first person singular, and it is Paul's attempt to cement as close a relationship between himself and the congregation as his rhetorical skills can deliver.

A Parenthetical Remark:
6:14–7:1

14Do not be misyoked with unbelievers. For what do righteousness and lawlessness have in common or what fellowship does light have with darkness? 15What harmony does Christ have with Beliar? Or what does believer share with unbeliever? 16What does a temple of God have in common with idols? For we are a temple of the living God. As God said,

> "I will dwell among them and walk in their midst
> And I will be their God
> And they will be my people." [Lev 26:12]
> 17Therefore, "Come out and be separated from among
>   them," says the Lord, "and do not touch the unclean,
>   [Isa 52:11]
> and I will receive you "[Ezek 20:34]

18And "I will be a father to you,
And you will be sons and daughters to me," [2 Sam 7:14]
     says the Lord Almighty.

7 1 Beloved, with these promises, therefore, let us cleanse ourselves from all defilement of the flesh and spirit, perfecting holiness in the fear of God.

As noted before, this passage violently interrupts the present literary context. It begins with a series of rhetorical questions (6:14–16d) that seem stylistically and materially so different from what has gone before and what will come next. The unmistakable rhetorical intent of these questions is to urge separation from unbelievers, defilement, darkness, and, by contrast, the embrace of believers, cleanliness, and light. As support for these actions, the passage adduces in 6:16d-18 a chain of scriptural quotations, Lev 26:12; Isa 52:11; Ezek 20:34; 2 Sam 7:14, none of which is cited exactly but all are arranged with a view of focusing on the Sinai covenant. If believers follow the advice of separating themselves from unbelievers, so goes the argument, they will be able to receive God's adoption (6:18) and the promises of God (7:1).

It is unclear what separation from "unbelievers" means. Many have taken it in general terms, counseling against commingling with members outside the Christian circle. Traditionally at least since the church father Cyprian, many have interpreted it as a prohibition against marrying unbelievers, but there is nothing in this particular passage that would prove or disprove such an interpretation. Still others take it to mean Paul's opponents. But the difficulty of identifying who the "unbelievers" are is indicative of the problem of interpreting the passage as a whole. There are ample reasons to question whether Paul is the author of this passage, and if he is not there would be no larger context within which to understand it.

First of all, we find a highly concentrated array of terms and ideas uncharacteristic of Paul in these few short verses. None of the Greek words behind the English "misyoked," "have in common" (6:14); "harmony," "Beliar" (6:15); "agreement" (6:16); "cleanse," "defilement" (7:1) can be found elsewhere in the undisputed letters of Paul. And if we take away the series of citations in 6:16c–18, every verse has at least one key term that is not used by Paul in any of his extant letters.

Secondly, there are key concepts in these verses that are

foreign, even inimical, to Paul's documented thinking. The uncompromising separation from "unbelievers" (6:14) seems contradictory to 1 Cor 5:10, where Paul corrects the Corinthians' misinterpretation of an earlier letter from him. The Corinthians had thought that when Paul wrote, "not to associate with sexually immoral persons," he meant immorality outside the church. But Paul corrects them by conceding that this would be impossible to do; what he means, in fact, is to be separate from false "brothers and sisters" who are sexually immoral. Likewise, in 1 Cor 7:12–16, Paul counsels that believers ought not be divorced from their unbelieving spouses. The thought behind the linked citation of Ezek 20:34 and 2 Sam 7:14 in 2 Cor 6:17d–18 is that the reception of God's promise of adoption is conditioned on their separation from uncleanliness. This conflicts openly with Paul's principal argument that God's promise is freely given. The prospect of believers being able to cleanse their own defilement on their own accord is also found nowhere else in the extant writings of Paul. The scriptural citations of verses 16–18 are delineated to glorify the Sinaitic covenant in which God established the Israelites as his people, but that seems to be the exact opposite of what Paul thought of the covenant in light of Gal 4:21–31, where Paul equates Sinai with slavery.

Finally, the thought world of 6:14–7:1 is redolent with sharp dualistic language. The unqualified dualistic language of light and darkness, believers versus unbelievers, God and idols, cleanliness and defilement, and finally body and spirit does not find a place in Paul, but is much more characteristic of the Qumran sectarians. For these reasons, it seems strongly persuasive that this passage did not originate with Paul.[18]

Chapter 5

The Collection for the Poor: 8:1–9:15

Towards the end of 2 Corinthians 7 Paul concludes his conciliatory letter on a note of confidence. He is now finished dealing
with the unpleasant business of his clash with a member of the
Corinthian church; he has explained, at least to his own satisfaction, the reason for his changed itinerary; now he can again turn
his mind to the collection for the Jerusalem church.[1] He does so
by first telling his readers that he is dispatching his trusted associate Titus to Corinth to oversee the collection effort. Titus,
he goes on, is greatly concerned for the affairs in Corinth: "His
heart goes out to you all the more." But he is no less an authoritative figure than Paul in spite of his compassion, for "he
remembers *the obedience* of all of you, how you received him
with *respect and trembling*" (7:15). The subtle reminder to the
Corinthians is that since they once showed respect to him, they
should continue to do so all the more. Paul tells the Corinthians
that he is sure they will not let him down, that they will make
good on his boast concerning them in front of Titus, just as they
have done before (7:14). Wielding carrot and stick, Paul ends his
appeal to the Corinthians, which also serves as preface to the
ensuing appeal for the collection (chapters 8–9).

We first encounter the collection in Gal 2:10 as part of Paul's
report on the Jerusalem Council. The Council had been con-
vened to discuss the question whether gentile converts would
have to be circumcised (Gal 2:1–2; Acts 15:1–5),[2] and it was resolved that the mission field be divided between Paul and the
so-called "reputed pillars" (Peter, James, and John), with the
latter in charge of ministry mainly among the Jews ("the circumcised"), and Paul to evangelize the "uncircumcised," that is, the

gentiles (Gal 2:7-9). Paul takes care to mention that nothing else was imposed on the gentiles — that is to say, the gentiles were not forcibly circumcised — only that "we remember the poor, which very thing I was also eager to do" (2:10).

This is a rather surprising interjection in itself, not the least because it pertains to nothing else that was reported as going on in Galatia and it stands out as a gratuitous piece of information in light of the controversy reflected in the whole letter. In 1 Cor 16:1 we do learn that Paul had instructed the Galatian churches about the collection, but that is never mentioned in the letter itself. More striking still, Paul shifts from the first person plural "*we* remember the poor" to the first person singular "which *I* was also eager to do" in the same sentence, as if to assume personal responsibility for the project. Reading this in hindsight after Paul had left Antioch (see Gal 2:11-14), this cannot be insignificant, nor can it be unintended. Paul and Barnabas had attended the meeting as official delegates from Antioch. At the conclusion of the meeting, according to Acts 15:22-29, the Council resolved, among other things, to reciprocate and send a delegate of its own to accompany Paul and Barnabas to Antioch with a formal report outlining its decision concerning the gentiles. From this we can see that the meeting was not so much an ecumenical council as it was a negotiation between the two leading churches of Jerusalem and Antioch, and the resolution reached thereby — including the collection — was a collective agreement between them. At the time of writing Galatians, however, Paul was no longer part of the Antioch church, after his public falling out with Peter and Barnabas and his departure from the city — in defeat in all likelihood. This means that by right he was no longer obligated to continue the collection; yet, he persisted in carrying it to its completion, in spite of personal cost. Why? There must have been deeply felt reasons that motivated him to do so.

One thing we can be quite certain of is that Paul did not think of the collection as a way of submitting the gentile churches to the supposed superiority of the Jerusalem church. The pillars' request for financial assistance from the Antioch church could well have been motivated by such an assumption; not only were they concerned for the needs of their church members, but it is possible that they also wanted to impose the authority of the mother church on the gentile population. But as we will see in greater detail, Paul understood well the Roman system of patron-client relationship which put the recipients of the gift in debt to the benefactors. If the question of authority was a consideration at all, the collection would render the Jerusalem church a client to their wealthier sister congregations in the diaspora.

An obvious reason for Paul to have expended so much energy on the collection was undoubtedly a genuine concern for the economic plights of the poor members in the Jerusalem church. From what we now know about the sociopolitical situation in the first century, Jerusalem was devoid of any significant industry or agricultural products. The one major attraction the city could offer was the temple, which generated income from visitors to the city for festivals and from religious offerings and alms-giving. The latter was understood to be especially meritorious when done in the Holy City. In addition, diaspora synagogues collected half a shekel from each adult male member to be sent to Jerusalem as temple tax. The city in general was there-fore reduced to depending on charity and benefaction from the outside.[3] Jerusalem Christians from all indications probably fared far worse than the populace in general. To what extent they participated in the temple cult and could derive economic benefits from it, is unclear from available sources. Jesus' no-toriety for anti-temple invectives could not have been helpful to their cause. But what we can be sure of is that there were persecutions and harassments; Paul himself confessed to having taken part in them (Gal 1:13, 23). This could not but make life difficult for the Christ-followers in a city in which religious au-thorities wielded enormous power. It is against this background that the Jerusalem pillars requested, and evidently were prom-ised, a collection for "the poor," and it is likely that economic hardship was one of the driving forces behind Paul's continual effort.

But it is possible that more is at stake for Paul, for as we will see in these two chapters he uses a plethora of theologically rich terms to describe the collection: grace, fellowship, ministry, ser-vice, and blessing. To say that Paul uses these as a device for fundraising would attribute an unduly cynical view that simply does not accord with his normal mode of operation, nor can it account for the personal sacrifices the apostle made for the completion of the project. To corroborate these preliminary ob-servations, the term "poor" admits of a rich variety of meanings. While it certainly refers to the sociopolitical condition, it can also mean the *eschatologically* poor. From the Dead Sea Scrolls unearthed in the 1950s, we learn that the Qumran sectarians also called themselves "the poor." While there is no doubt that economic hardship stands at the heart of the problem, not all of the Jerusalem church can be called materially poor, as Rom 15:26, "the poor *among* the saints," attests. But this last point is precisely why a part of the Jerusalem church, mostly likely among its leadership, would have to understand "poor" in the eschatological sense if they used it as a self-designation at all.[4] Whatever their self-understanding might have been, there are theological dimensions to Paul's collection effort, which is why he seemed so eager to integrate this into his missionary work.

Second Corinthians 8–9 does not represent Paul's first attempt to appeal to the Corinthians to contribute to the collection for Jerusalem. In 8:6, 10, Paul refers to a "beginning" of the Corinthian effort that took place "last year." In 1 Cor 16:1–4, Paul is already answering questions about the collection which the Corinthians had for him, questions Chloe's people had reported to Paul most likely, along with other pressing questions (see 1 Cor 1:11; 5:1; 7:1). In 1 Cor 16:2, the questions appear to have to do with the method of collection. Paul advises the Corinthians — as he has done the same to the Galatian church[5] — that each is to plan on putting aside and saving up extra money every Sunday for the effort (verses 1–2). In the same context, he also mentions in passing that he plans to go to Corinth after going to Macedonia (verse 3),[6] which makes it probable that his trip through Macedonia, visiting churches in Philippi, Thessalonica, and perhaps Beroea, was for the same purpose of coordinating the collection effort. The mention of Timothy in verse 10 would lead one to think that he was the person designated to supervise the job. Since Paul has to advise the Corinthians to plan their giving extra every week, it would be an indication that the Corinthians, while certainly better off than their Jerusalem brothers and sisters, were not inordinately wealthy. Paul has to rely on planned giving rather than on ready monies for the collection.[7]

At the time of writing 1 Corinthians, Paul did not seem to be aware that there might be serious doubts about the collection. Paul's directive appears to be rather straightforward: it deals merely with the administrative aspects of the project rather than with any possible suspicion that might have been raised about it. This would soon change, however. As we have seen in chapter 3, Paul at one point proposed to visit the Corinthians twice, most probably because of his concerns for the collection, but his later change of itinerary had caused some complaints from the Corinthians (1:15–17). Furthermore, several times in 2 Corinthians Paul defends himself and his associates against the charge of "taking advantage of" the Corinthians (7:2; 12:17–18). All this is fair indication that at least some members of the Corinthian church have insinuated that this collection effort was but a front for Paul's personal gain. Someone might have suggested that even though Paul had refused to accept financial assistance from the church officially, he nevertheless insisted upon asking them for financial contributions — under the guise of almsgiving.

In spite of the obstacles, Titus and the unnamed "brothers" of chapters 8 and 9 made the trip to Corinth, but that evidently succeeded only in arousing more suspicions and misunderstandings. In 12:17–18 (part of Letter D), Paul has to clear himself, as well as Titus and "the brother," of charges of fraud. After the dust had settled, Paul evidently took a trip to coordinate the effort personally and he somehow managed to complete the collection. This he recounts in Rom 15:25–27: Macedonia and Achaia have completed the collection, and he would make the trip to Jerusalem accompanying the gift.[8] This account, unfortunately, still leaves us guessing as to how Paul finally convinced the Corinthians to make their contribution to the collection. We will return to the fate of the collection at the end of this chapter.

Given the suspicions the collection has aroused among the Corinthians, it is all the more remarkable that Paul was able to persist to the end, evidently until its eventual completion. And it certainly makes us that much more curious about our question regarding the basis for Paul's strong conviction about and commitment to the project. To answer this question and to ferret out Paul's theological interpretation of his relief effort, we will have to look more closely at 2 Corinthians 8–9, his most extensive comments on the collection among his surviving letters.

Good Work as Grace; Capacity for the Collection: 8:1–15

8 [1]We want to inform you, brothers and sisters, of the grace of God which has been given to the churches of Macedonia,

²because in a severe trial of affliction, the abundance of their joy and their rock-bottom poverty have overflowed into the wealth of their generosity. ³For they were able — and, I witness, even beyond what they were able — out of their own initiative ⁴to implore us most insistently⁹ for a favor of participating¹⁰ in the ministry for the saints. ⁵And — not as we expected — they gave themselves first of all to the Lord and, by the will of God, to us. ⁶We say this, in order to urge Titus that just as he had made a beginning, so he might also complete it for the sake of you and of this generous gift.¹¹ ⁷But just as you abound in everything — in faith, in speech, in knowledge, in great eagerness, and in the love from us among you — so you may abound also in this act of generous gift.¹²

⁸I say this not as a command but through the eagerness of others; I also want to test the genuineness of your love. ⁹For you know the generous gift¹³ of our Lord, Jesus Christ, that he, though rich, became poor for your sake, so that through his poverty you may become rich. ¹⁰And regarding this matter let me give you my opinion: For this is beneficial to you who started this last year, not only the task but also the desire in doing it. ¹¹Now, then, complete the task, so that your true desire¹⁴ might be matched by the completion of the task out of what you have. ¹²For if the true desire is present, it is acceptable on the basis of what one has, not on what one does not have. ¹³For it is not a matter of relief to others and affliction to you, but it is a matter of equality. ¹⁴At present, your abundance is for their deficit, so that their abundance may be for your deficit as well. All this is for the sake of equality. ¹⁵As it is written, "The one who had much did not have too much, and the one who had little did not have too little" [Exod 16:18].

What follows amounts to a solicitation letter to the Corinthians for money, yet Paul does not actually begin with a direct appeal to them. Instead, he opens with an encapsulated *résumé* of the Macedonian success story (8:1–5) before he tells his readers that he is sending Titus to complete the collection (verse 6) — all this in one sentence! The intent here, as we have become familiar with Paul's rhetorical strategy, has to do with how Paul constructs a problem for his readers to which the rest of chapters 8–9 is a solution, and the problem is one of competition between the Corinthians and the churches in Philippi, Thessalonica, and perhaps even Beroea.¹⁵ Earlier in our discussion of

Paul's change of itinerary in 1:15-16, going first to Macedonia before coming to Corinth (see chapter 3), we saw the growing jealousy of the Corinthian church for what they perceived to be Paul's preferential treatment of their northern compatriots. This was no doubt fueled by Paul's willingness to accept financial assistance from the congregations in Philippi and his refusal to be supported by the Corinthians (cf. also 1 Cor 9:8-18; 2 Cor 12:13). Paul could not have been totally ignorant of all this,[16] and he uses it here in the hope of goading the Corinthians into following through with their year-long pledge to contribute to the collection.

If competition is the rhetorical problem, however, it is more than a little surprising that his proposed solution to the problem does not make any reference to it. He does not prop up the Macedonian success as a model for the Corinthians to emulate, nor does he advocate open competition with them. Instead, he reminds the Corinthians what they have done. In 8:6, he tells his readers that he is sending Titus to finish what they have already started, in fact, "since last year" (verse 10). And in 8:7, he enumerates for them the gifts they abound in, suggesting that they should "abound also in this grace."[17] Paul could have said all this *without* first bringing up the Macedonians. Or could he? The answer to that would of course depend on what exactly Paul has said about the Macedonians.

In the opening sentence, Paul says, "We want to inform you, brothers and sisters, of the grace of God which has been given to the churches of Macedonia, because in a severe trial of affliction, the abundance of their joy and their rock-bottom poverty have overflowed into the wealth of their generosity" (8:1-2). The affliction mentioned here is probably the same as that Paul says he has experienced himself in 7:5, and that may well have caused the "rock-bottom poverty" that they are suffering. Philippi and Thessalonica were prosperous cities on the Via Egnatia; the church's poverty there must have been the result of harassment or localized persecution. In any case, Paul uses this fact to stress the overflowing wealth of their generosity. In spite of their impoverished conditions, Paul goes on, the Macedonians were able nonetheless to make a generous contribution, and the next verse tells us that they even went beyond their means in their support for the relief project (verse 3). But what is crucial for his appeal to the Corinthians later — indeed, what paves the way for it — is that Paul does not attribute any of this to the personal qualities of the Macedonians; he attributes it to "the *grace of God* which has been given" to them (verse 1).

"Grace" or "gift" (Greek, *charis*) is Paul's leading term for the collection. In these two chapters, Paul uses a whole host of equally rich terms in connection with the collection: *eulogia* ("blessing") four times, in 9:5 (twice), 9:6 (twice); *diakonia* ("ministry") four times, in 8:4; 9:1, 12, 13; *leitourgia* ("religious service") once, in 9:12; and *koinōnia* ("fellowship") twice, in 8:4; 9:13. Elsewhere he uses the same vocabulary: in Rom 15:25–27, he describes it as "ministry to the saints" (using the verb *diakonoun* in verse 25), "fellowship" or "sharing" (*koinōnia*, verse 26), "service" (*leitourgein*, verse 26). By contrast, only once in all his references to the collection does Paul use a non-theological, commercial term, "contribution" (Greek, *legeia*, 1 Cor 16:1, 2), to describe the collection.

But his favorite term remains "grace," which is used ten times in these two chapters alone, 8:1, 4, 6, 7, 9, 16, 19; 9:8, 14, 15, and once more in 1 Cor 16:3, and is variously translated here as "generous gift," "favor," as well as simply "grace." It is impossible to translate the Greek *charis* consistently in this passage, since it is used to mean different things, but it cannot be accidental that Paul chooses to use the same term for these various purposes. In fact, he begins chapter 8 with a reference to the grace of God. The word could be used actively, meaning a favor one bestows upon others. This is most likely the meaning in verse 4, where the Macedonians beseech Paul for the opportunity to take part in the collection; *charis* in this regard is the favor that Paul could bestow on them. Thus the NRSV rightly translates it as "privilege." This is apparently also how the term is used in verse 6 ("We [urged] Titus that just as he had made a beginning, so he might also complete it for the sake of you and of this *generous gift*"); *charis* here means simply the "gift" that the Corinthians were about to bestow on the Jerusalem saints.

But *charis* can also be used passively, as something experienced as a gift from another person, notably God, and this is how it is used in verse 1. "The grace of God" given to the Macedonians is a gift received from God. It is because the Macedonians first received this grace that they were able to contribute to the Jerusalem church with such spectacular success. As a result, the Macedonians are praised for giving "*themselves* to the Lord and to us" (verse 5). While one would obviously place the stress on the total sum of the donation, which after all is the desired outcome of a collection effort, Paul stresses what the gift also symbolizes: namely, the Macedonians' giving of themselves. By implication, therefore, God is the prime giver who has made givers out of the Macedonians. Now it becomes clear why Paul uses the Macedonians as example: it is because they exercise their gifts from God that they have been empowered and enabled to become contributors to the collection. One becomes a giver because one has first received a gift.

This gift-giver relationship is Paul's message to the Corinthians as well. He begins developing this theme more fully in verse 7: "But just as you abound in everything — in faith, in speech, in knowledge, in great eagerness, and in the love from us among you — so you may abound also in this act of generous gift (Greek, *charis*)." Faith, speech, knowledge, and love are all spiritual gifts which Paul has already mentioned in 1 Corinthians (12:8–9; 13:1). In addition, he praised the Corinthians for abounding in "speech and knowledge of every sort" (1 Cor 1:5). Spiritual gifts (Greek, *charismata*) literally mean "things received as a result of divine grace (Greek, *charis*)." According to Paul they are bestowed freely on the believer by the Spirit, as a result of which they could fulfill such extraordinary acts as miracles, speaking in tongues, prophecy, spiritual insights. If the Corinthians abound in these gifts — as Paul knows, that is something they take great pride in — they ought also to abound in the grace that is capable of producing overflowing wealth of generosity. If the problem constructed by Paul destabilizes the Corinthians' sense of themselves by driving a wedge between them and the Macedonians, his appeal to the productive dimension of grace bridges the gap and maintains continuity between these two congregations. If competition is the problem, Paul proposes that the solution is to discern what makes the Macedonians so successful. Stressing the commonality the Corinthians have with the Macedonians, Paul surmises, may turn out to be more productive than focusing on their separation induced by their competitiveness.

If the motive for supporting the collection is found within the experience of the spiritual gifts, one can say Paul is not imposing a command on the Corinthians. All such giving has to be voluntary and cannot be imposed from without; thus every good deed, if it is to be called moral at all, must be generated by its own imperative and not be enticed or pressured by outside influences. He makes the same point when he tries to persuade Philemon to take the runaway slave Onesimus back: though he could well command him to do so, he would much rather leave it to the latter's voluntary acceptance of the wayward slave that is based purely on love (Philem 8–9). But of course, by saying that he would not impose a command, Paul makes it known that he in fact does have the apostolic authority to do so, even if he chooses not to exercise it. It is enough to allude to the threat of power — it is certainly far more effective — than to use it. Paul's rhetorical intent in 2 Cor 8:8 is no different.

Besides his emphasis on the moral imperative of every ethical deed, Paul's decision not to command the Corinthians to take part in the collection is also a consequence of his placing it within the context of spiritual gifts. Paul is convinced that the active participation in the relief effort must be part of the Corinthians' spiritual experience and the natural outcome of their gifts. The collection is an occasion to show that these spiritual gifts are genuinely received. Insofar as the granting of these gifts depends on divine prerogatives and not on human initiatives, therefore, Paul cannot say that they could be developed or strengthened through self-effort, and a command in this regard would be out of place. But insofar as the collection is an occasion to put these gifts into practice — or in the language of verse 8, to test whether they are genuine or not — it is legitimate to demand human attention. That is why the Macedonians could beseech Paul (literally, "to plead with much appealing") for the "grace" to take part in the collection (8:4). By the same token, how the Corinthians respond to Paul's call would also be an indication whether they have received the true spiritual gifts at all — namely, love. Elsewhere in 1 Cor 12:31, Paul has already made clear that the most excellent of all spiritual gifts is love (so in 8:8).

In support of this exhortation, Paul's introduces his next statement, a most unique Christological confession that has spilled much scholarly ink, "for you know the grace of our Lord, Jesus Christ, that he, though rich, became poor for your sake, so that through his poverty you may become rich" (verse 9). This confession is unique, because nowhere else in the New Testament is Christ portrayed in terms of this rich-poor antithesis. It does not help us to think back to the historical Jesus who as an artisan would not be in dire poverty. Paul in any case does not show a consistent interest in the earthly life and career of Jesus, at least not so far as we can tell from his letters, and there is no indication that he is appealing to the earthly Jesus for inspiration here. It is possible that Paul is here thinking of the incarnation in close parallel to the famous Philippian Hymn, "He possessed the form of God, ... but he emptied himself taking the form of a servant" (Phil 2:6–7), so that being rich is equated to having the form of God and being poor to taking the form of a servant. The problem with this interpretation is that Paul cites the confession in order to apply it to the Corinthians, " ... so that through his poverty *you may become rich.*" In that case, for the Corinthians to become rich they would have to take on the form of God, which is unlikely to be what Paul intends to say, here or anywhere.[18]

The closest correspondence to the kind of exchange and substitution formulated in verse 9 is found in 2 Corinthians itself in the statement, "[God] made [Christ] sin who knew no sin on our behalf, in order that we might become the righteousness of God through him" (5:21). As we saw earlier in chapter 4, this is a classic expression of substitutionary atonement according to which Christ, the righteousness of God, was identified with sin ("[God] made him sin"), so that our sins might be taken away and we might become the righteousness of God. By this analogy, being rich is equated to the righteousness of God and being poor to sin. But how does Christ in fact become identified with sin? According to 5:14–15, he accomplished all this through his death, by dying for all, and this death is an expression of love. This expansion on the idea of substitutionary atonement in terms of love corresponds closely to Paul's intention in chapter 8. He exhorts the Corinthians to take the collection as an opportunity, precisely to test their love (verse 8). To undergird this exhortation he uses the example of Christ's love manifested in his death for all. As a result of Christ's love, as a result of Christ's having been changed from righteousness to sin — that is, from riches to poverty — believers have been changed from sin to righteousness, from poverty to riches. In line with this interpretation, "the grace of our Lord Jesus Christ" accordingly means the love of Christ. This is consistent with how Paul uses "grace" earlier in chapter 8 to refer to the most excellent spiritual gift of all, love, which must stand behind the collection effort.

Paul is suggesting to the Corinthians in verses 8–9, therefore, that they emulate the example of Christ's love: divest their riches for the sake of others, just as Christ has done the same for them, so that others may become rich as a result. In so doing, Paul reminds his Corinthian readers of their salvation and asks them to concretize their spiritual well-being in the material sphere of their lives. This means, at the present time, fulfilling their responsibilities towards the material well-being of their impoverished brothers and sisters in Jerusalem.

It is in this sense of concretizing their spiritual gift of love that Paul means when he says that finishing the collection is "beneficial" to the Corinthians (verse 10). The same understanding also stands behind Paul's urgent appeal to the Corinthians to finish what they started (verse 11). While the desire to do the job is commendable, it is action that finally counts. Just as the love of Christ demonstrates its completion, its perfection, in his dying for all, the love of Corinthians can be demonstrated only when they have completed the task of the contribution.

Love is the most excellent gift in Paul's estimation because it builds up the body of Christ. Christians follow the example of Christ's love only insofar as it is done *for the sake of others*. In verses 12–14, Paul reiterates the same theme, but this time he does so using a new notion, equality. Giving is done on the basis of "what one has, not what one does not have" (verse 12). Some have rightly called this "proportional giving," that is to take the contribution out of what one has in surplus. It is clear that Paul does not attach any absolute virtue to "poverty," as if such an affliction entitles the afflicted to special treatment. If anything, the use of the rich-poor antithesis to understand the atoning death of Christ derives coherent meaning only if being rich is assumed to be something desirable and being poor something undesirable. Here, he takes care to debunk the notion that "relief to others" must mean "affliction" to the givers (verse 13a). The kind of asceticism or self-renunciation that developed later in church history finds no support here.

But lest his readers commit the opposite error, that of overvaluing wealth, Paul immediately follows up with the comment that the bottom-line criterion for evaluating whether or not one has done the right thing with the money is equality (verses 13b–14). Surplus has to be understood not as an absolute good in itself but as something to be evaluated in conjunction with those in need. The Corinthians, modest in material means as they undoubtedly were, were nevertheless in abundance when compared to the Jerusalem congregation. The principle of equality then dictates that they ought to advance their abundance toward making up the deficits of the poorer members of the same body. In like manner, if the situation were the reverse, the abundance of others would also be marshaled to make up for any deficiency of the Corinthians. Later in Rom 15:25–27 Paul would develop equality into the notion that gentiles receive the "spiritual blessing" from the Jewish Christians. Here, however, there is not yet any evidence that Paul has this idea in mind. In support of this sense of equality, Paul cites in verse 15 the story of picking manna in the wilderness in Exodus. Every Israelite is allowed to pick one day's supply of manna, yet every person has enough according to his or her needs, so that "the one who had much did not have too much, and the one who had little did not have too little" (Exod 16:18). Everyone's needs are thereby satisfied. Equality, finally, does not mean sameness but is realized in proportion to what everyone needs.

This close reading of 8:1–15 has given us at least one answer to our earlier question why Paul expended so much of his energy on the collection effort for the Jerusalem church. It is because such a collection effort is a logical consequence of his understanding that the church is the body of Christ. The Jerusalem Council might have resolved the problem of dividing the mission field between the circumcised and the uncircumcised, but it did not anticipate the potential problems created by such a sharp division. As Paul's mission among gentiles became more and more successful, and as well-to-do churches were being founded one by one, he realized that the relief effort for the impoverished congregations in Jerusalem stipulated by the Council could well be used to foster a unity between Jewish and gentile believers. Not only was it politic for him to do so, but this perception also sprang directly from his theology of the body of Christ. As such, the collection became a validation of his whole theology.

Paul is no armchair theologian, however, who is blind to political machination that inevitably emerges whenever a large sum of money is involved. In presenting to the Corinthians a theology of corporate unity standing behind his appeal for the collection, Paul is also keenly aware of the need to put in place an administrative apparatus that is not only efficient but also above reproach and suspicion. This he details in the following passage.

Administration Apparatus for the Collection;
An Advance Party to Corinth: 8:16–9:5

8 ¹⁶Thanks be to God who put the same eagerness for you in Titus's heart, ¹⁷for as he received our appeal, he, being so very eager, took the initiative in going to you. ¹⁸We sent with him the brother whose fame in the gospel is known throughout all the churches, ¹⁹and who, moreover, was handpicked by the churches as our travel companion, accompanying this gift administered by us, for the glory of the Lord and our goodwill. ²⁰We are doing this so that no one would accuse us regarding this generosity administered by us. ²¹For we take heed of good things, not only before God but also before human beings. ²²We sent with them our brother whom we have tested, on many occasions and often, to be eager — now more eager because of his great confidence in you. ²³As for Titus, he is my partner and coworker for you; as for our brothers, they are apostles of the churches, a glory of Christ. ²⁴Therefore demonstrate to them before the churches the proof of your love and of our boast on your behalf.

9 ¹So, even though it is superfluous for me to write to you regarding the ministry to the saints — ²for I know your eagerness of which I boast, on your behalf, to the Macedonians: namely, Achaia has been prepared since last year, and your zeal has roused many of them — ³I nevertheless sent the brothers, in order that our boast for you might not prove empty in this respect, and that you would be ready just as I was saying, ⁴lest somehow if the Macedonians came with me and found you unprepared, we — to say nothing of you — would be put to shame in this undertaking. ⁵Therefore, I thought it necessary to exhort the brothers that they go to you and prepare ahead of time the blessing you promised, that it may be ready as a blessing and not an extortion.

There has been much scholarly debate on the question whether chapter 9 is a separate letter or whether it is part of the same letter as chapter 8. It has been pointed out that the opening verses in this chapter are unnecessarily repetitive. They seem to introduce the whole topic of the collection all over again, as if chapter 8 (especially verse 4) did not exist (9:1). The introductory sentence, literally "Concerning *the ministry to the saints* . . . ," also seems to read like one of Paul's customary formulas signaling a new topic (see, for example, 1 Cor 7:1, 25; 8:1; 12:1; 16:1; 1 Thess 4:9; 5:1). Moreover, after using the Macedonians as example to spur the Corinthians on (8:1–5), Paul in 9:2 seems to use *the Corinthians* to inspire the Macedonians to action: " ... I know your eagerness of which I boast, on your behalf, to the Macedonians: namely, Achaia has been prepared since last year, and your zeal has roused many of them." On the basis of these two considerations, many scholars have argued that chapter 9 was originally an independent composition, perhaps intended as a circular letter to Achaians outside the capital city of Corinth.

All these are strong arguments, but there are stronger arguments still for taking chapter 9 as a continuation of Paul's appeal to the Corinthian church that begins in chapter 8. Though 9:1 appears to repeat the topic of collection already stated in 8:4, the latter is, strictly speaking, not a direct appeal to the Corinthians but a report of what the Macedonian Christians have besought Paul for: "imploring us with much insistence for the grace and fellowship connected with the *ministry for the saints*." While it does indirectly introduce the topic of the collection, it is not a direct appeal to the Corinthians. As a matter of fact, there is no appeal for the collection at all in the whole of chapter 8, in which Paul only alludes to the need for the Corinthians to exercise their spiritual gift of love to the fullest, to Christ's giving up of himself, to the responsibility of completing what they started, to the principle of equality—but otherwise he makes no mention of the collection. "It is superfluous for me to write to you regarding the ministry to the saints" (9:1) is therefore the first instance in these two chapters in which Paul explicitly connects the Corinthians to the collection. Furthermore, even 9:1 itself is not an appeal as such but a rhetorical set up for the next four verses: It is both an opening for Paul to tell the Corinthians about what the Macedonians expect of them, because he has boasted on their behalf (verse 2), and a justification for sending "the brothers" to Corinth (verses 3–5).[19] In this respect, the opening sentence is not a formula introducing a new topic but a continuation of his earlier discussion of sending Titus and the two brothers (8:16–24).[20]

As to the second argument that Paul in 9:2 holds up the Corinthians as example to the Macedonians, this is really not that different from what Paul does in 8:1–5. There he uses the Macedonian success to challenge the Corinthians; here he uses the Macedonian expectation, engineered by himself no less, to

wake the Corinthians from their stupor of irresponsibility and
to pressure them into fulfilling their forgotten promises. In both
cases, he uses the same underlying competition between these
two provinces as motivation for the Corinthians to act. The spur
might be different, but the same delivery jolts no less.

In fact, there are various aspects of chapter 9 that presuppose chapter 8. Most noticeably, the sending of "the brothers"
in 9:3, 5 would make no sense unless it is read against the
foregoing section of 8:16–24. The brothers' mission to Corinth
mentioned in both these passages appears different at first. The
statement in 8:20, "We are doing this so that no one would accuse us regarding this generosity administered by us," implies
that one of the brothers' functions is to make sure that nothing untoward would happen to the contribution – no doubt
reflecting again the persistent suspicion of Paul's handling of finances. In 9:5, on the other hand, the brothers are described
as going to Corinth to make sure that the collection (which
is called "blessing" here) is prepared in time for Paul to col-
lect and for the Macedonians to witness (9:4). But surely these
two concerns are not mutually exclusive and both could be fulfilled by the same mission. Furthermore, the policing of the
collection is the responsibility of only one of the brothers, the
one mentioned in 8:18. The other unnamed brother, not mentioned until 8:22, is one of Paul's own ("our brother whom we
have tested"); there is no reason why he could not carry out
the task of preparing the collection before Paul's arrival. In all,
there are no compelling reasons to detach chapter 9 from the
rest of the letter, but there are strong arguments to the contrary. It is better to consider chapter 9 as part of Paul's appeal
to the Corinthians for the collection. And since 9:1–5 continues the description of the brothers' mission, it is here grouped
together with 8:16–24. The last section, 9:6–15, concludes the
whole letter of appeal.

Given the amount of space devoted to Titus and the two unnamed brothers in 8:16–9:5, which occupies nearly half of the
letter, it is not difficult to see that chapters 8–9, if they constitute a unity, are basically a letter of recommendation for the
emissaries being sent to Corinth. Titus's prominence in the letter of reconciliation (see, for example, 2:13; 7:6, 13b–16) and his
continual presence here would lead to the natural conclusion
that he is the letter carrier and the leader of the group. Earlier

in 8:6, he is introduced as being commissioned by Paul and his colleagues to supervise the collection. There Paul puts the onus explicitly on Titus, for since he started the project, now he must bring it to completion. But the implicit burden is actually placed on the Corinthians, because as emerges in verses 10–12, it is the Corinthians who have not kept up the earlier promise they made in spite of what must have been an initial enthusiasm for the project. The fuller introduction of Titus in 8:16–17 and 23 makes no further mention of the Corinthian tardiness, only that he is eager to take the initiative upon himself for the job (verses 16–17), and that he is Paul's partner and co-worker (verse 23). All this would indicate that Titus is intended by Paul as his personal representative, to be accorded full authority and respect by the Corinthians.

The first unnamed brother is described as renowned to all the churches (8:18). He is handpicked by presumably the same churches to be part of Paul's entourage as they go from church to church soliciting funds for the collection and maybe also when they transport the completed collection to Jerusalem (verse 19). Who these churches are Paul keeps mysteriously silent, but since this famous brother has built his reputation on the gospel, that is, on preaching and missionary work (verse 18), he is presumably not a local leader but someone widely recognized in all the major cities, someone perhaps not unlike Paul himself. In describing the conveyance of the diaspora tribute to the Jerusalem temple — a complicated logistic problem when such a large sum is involved — Philo informs us that only the most meritorious and men of the highest repute from every city would be selected to be part of the envoy.[21] The "famous brother" is clearly someone of that caliber. As to why so famous a preacher would remain nameless, our text yields no definitive answers, but Acts 20:4 does mention three persons from Macedonia and two from Asia who accompany Paul to Jerusalem with the collection. It is possible that one of those named is our "famous brother."

But our text does tell us why such a widely known person of high repute is chosen for the trip. Paul says in verses 20–21, somewhat wryly, "We are doing this so that no one would accuse us regarding this generosity administered by us. For we take heed of good things not only before God but also before human beings." As we have seen, Paul is ever vigilant concerning the Corinthian suspicion that he might be misappropriating for his personal gain the funds for the collection. To head off this charge, even before his own arrival, he is inviting someone who is above reproach and who is selected not by him but by all the churches to travel with him — as witness. All this might be unnecessary, he implies in his paraphrase of Prov 3:4 in verse 21, for he is open and honest "before God"; but he wants it known that he is also shrewd enough to know that a pure motive may not be enough in financial matters and has to be supplemented by human witness. But it is also possible that Paul wants to apply subtle pressure on the Corinthians by including someone who is widely known. After the introduction of the three representatives, Paul asks the Corinthians to demonstrate their love "before the churches" (verse 24). Similarly in 9:2, 4, Paul mentions the Macedonian high expectation of the Corinthians in their collection effort. The not-so-subtle message to the Corinthians is that all the churches are watching and waiting. And the presence of the famous brother makes this pressure visible.

The third member of the envoy, also unnamed, is introduced in verse 22. He is described as tested and earnest. His role is less clearly defined, except that he is from Paul's company, since he is called "our brother." Judged by the lack of information about him, he is probably not known to the Corinthians. As the last-named, he must have played only a subordinate role to that of Titus.

The responsibilities of those chosen delegates seem at first perfunctory. Paul's request in 8:24 that Titus and the brothers be received into the Corinthian church adds nothing new. The language, "proof of your love," consciously recalls "the genuineness of your love" in 8:8, although it can at the same time mean love to the three visitors. But it is in 9:1–5 that we get a fuller picture of the task that awaits them. As we have seen earlier, Paul puts a good deal of pressure on the Corinthians by once again bringing the Macedonians into the picture. The Corinthians not only have to perform under the distant watchful eyes of the Macedonians, to whom Paul had boasted of the former's effort in the collection (9:2); now, according to 9:4, they will have to answer to Macedonian visitors whom Paul is threatening to bring when he comes. This cannot make for a tranquil time for the Corinthians, and the collection could be seen not as a free-will offering but, as Paul anticipates it in 9:5, as "an extortion." All this cannot but result in an exceedingly difficult job for Titus and the two brothers. They are charged with bringing the collection to completion *before* Paul comes and therefore in his absence; as Paul's representatives, they will bear the brunt of the Corinthians' invectives but will not have Paul's presence to back up their authority; and given the sensitive situation in Corinth, these men will have to play both fund managers and skillful negotiators. While Titus is familiar with the Corinthian congregation's difficult relationship with Paul, the two brothers are clearly not known to the Corinthians and may not be prepared to discharge their responsibilities. Right from the start, the success of their mission is in doubt. As we will see in 12:17-18, the mission of the delegates indeed failed. Given all the unfavorable odds against it, it was perhaps inevitable that it did.

Good Work as Harvest;
Rewards for the Collection:
9:6–15

⁶This is the saying, "One who sows sparingly also reaps sparingly, and one who sows bountifully also reaps bountifully." ⁷Each must give as each chooses in the heart, not grudgingly or under compulsion, for God loves a cheerful giver. ⁸God is able to increase every grace in abundance for you, so that, being self-sufficient in everything in every circumstance always, you may abound for every good work. ⁹As it is written, "He scattered abroad, he gave to the needy, his righteousness abides forever" [Ps 112:9]. ¹⁰He who supplies seed to the sower and bread for food will supply and multiply your seed and increase the yield of your righteousness.

¹¹In everything, you are being made rich for the purpose of every act of generosity, which produces thanksgiving to God through us. ¹²For the ministry of this service not only supplies the deficits of the saints but also abounds in many thanksgivings to God. ¹³You glorify God through the test of this ministry because of the obedience of your confession of the Gospel of God and because of the generosity of your sharing with them and with everyone, ¹⁴while they with prayer on your behalf long for you on account of the surpassing grace of God upon you. ¹⁵Thanks be to God for his indescribable gift!

After assembling an administrative team to coordinate the collection in advance of his arrival, Paul now concludes his appeal by elaborating on the theological foundation for giving. If chapters 8 and 9 belong together, as we have argued that they do, then 9:6–15 recapitulates the theology of grace first adumbrated in 8:1–15, furthers it by adding a new element of thanksgiving to that theology, and finally concludes the whole appeal on a note of optimism.

We recall that in 8:1–5 Paul deliberately formulates the collection as an effort issued from the "grace of God" (8:1), and he uses the self-giving of Christ out of his love for humanity (the "generous gift of our Lord Jesus Christ" in 8:9) as an example to motivate the Corinthians to participate in this undertaking. God is the primary giver who creates a capacity in the believers so that they in turn become givers themselves. As part of the same emphasis on the divine initiative in giving, Paul also reminds his readers of their reception of such spiritual gifts as faith, speech, knowledge, and love (8:8). There is a definite parallel, then, between the reception of spiritual gifts (Greek, *charisma*) and the reception of divine grace (Greek, *charis*). Generous giving turns out to be an extension of divine grace, and that could be seen as the exercise of spiritual gifts — both grace and spiritual gifts are ultimately traceable to the divine initiative. Here in 9:6–15, Paul extends and concretizes this earlier argument of his: The act of giving stems not from human self, as if by self effort one could acquire a spirit of generosity, but ultimately from God.

Paul begins this passage with a common Jewish saying found in a variety of Wisdom texts, "One who sows sparingly also reaps sparingly, and one who sows bountifully also reaps bountifully" (verse 6),[22] which at first sight reads like a calculating piece of commercialism. It is as if Paul were trying to motivate the Corinthians by dangling some reward, some bountiful harvest before them, as if he were suggesting that they look at the collection as a wise investment that would some day yield a high return upon its maturity. This initial suspicion is deepened as we read further on. Paul continues the agricultural imagery in the following verses but continues his emphasis on the yields of one's moral behavior. In verse 8, Paul says that as a result of cheerful giving, God will "*increase every grace* in abundance" in the lives of the givers. In verse 10, drawing out implications from his citation of Ps 112:9 in the last verse, he tells his readers that good work will prompt God to "*supply and multiply* your seed and *increase your yield* of righteousness." It seems inescapable to conclude that the apostle is here working with a reward-oriented calculus and not the moral purity of the action itself. This seems contrary to what we have suggested to be the reason why Paul refuses to command the Corinthians to take part in the collection (8:8), which is to focus on the purely moral character of the work and not to comply merely because of external pressure. Can Paul here be accused of being mercenary?

First, we need to examine what makes something mercenary. It is mercenary if, for example, one seeks public office for monetary gains or gives alms for the sake of personal fame. Both of these cases can legitimately be called mercenary, not because the actions produce rewards, be it financial or personal, but because the rewards do not correspond with or conform to the original intents of the actions. The purpose of a public office is the service of the people not money, and the goal of philanthropy is the benefits of others not oneself. In both examples, the more lofty aim of an action is replaced by a lesser one, one unintended by the action itself. If, on the other hand, one looks for financial gains by investing in the stock market or seeks fame by being a world-famous explorer, the money and fame one gets as a result would not render the pursuits mercenary but make them successful ones. One might quibble with the original intents of these pursuits, as an authoritarian and collectivist society that derogates personal fame and fortunes would, but it would not be wrong or unethical to focus on the results. These actions are not mercenary in spite of the personal nature of the results they produce, because they are taken precisely for the purpose of producing such results. In fact, the better the results, the more successful is the enterprise.

So it is with Paul's argument in 9:6–15. Paul does structure the collection in terms of actions and rewards, but he does so all within the context of sowing and reaping bountifully (verse 6). But what in fact does one sow or reap? Verse 8 gives us a clue: "God is able to increase every *grace* in abundance for you, so that, being self-sufficient in everything in every circumstance always, you may abound for every *good work*." What we are supplied with is "grace," and what that grace produces is "good work." Good work in this context means, of course, the generous contribution to the collection project. Self-sufficiency was an ancient philosophical ideal of independence and abundance, and Paul obviously uses the concept here to speak of financial and material abundance. But in Paul's grace-centered calculus, self-sufficiency is nothing more than a middle-term between grace and good work. The Corinthians have been well provided for materially, which is a clear sign of divine grace, but material abundance is not the ultimate end, good work is. God has given much to the Corinthians, so that they could in turn use their financial resources to produce more good work. So, while Paul does call the Corinthians' attention to the outcome of their action, that outcome turns out to be the very thing intended by the action all along. Grace produces abundance, but the abundance is finally meant for good work.

We should understand verses 9–10 in the same light. Verse 9 is a citation of Ps 112:9, originally a psalm in praise of the righteous person: "He scattered abroad, he gave to the needy, his righteousness abides forever." But Paul supplies an interpretation in verse 10 that leaves one with no doubt that he has changed the subject of the sentence from the righteous man to God, "He [that is, God] who supplies seed to the sower and bread for food will supply and multiply your seed and increase the yield of your righteousness." It can only be God who is in a position to increase one's righteousness. This change is deliberate: Paul wants to emphasize that a righteous man acts only insofar as God acts in him. If a person sows seeds in the field, it is God who first supplies the human subject with the seeds, and if the person gives food to the needy, it is God who first provides the food. But as the righteous person does these good works, God will multiply the seeds and increase the measure of righteousness. "Righteousness," in accordance with Jewish exegesis of the first century, refers to good work. The result is a kind of ethical truism: one does good work, so that one can increase further one's capacity to do more good work. Paul's point here, accordingly, is essentially the same as that of verse 8. That is why the voluntary giving "as a cheerful giver" is important in this context (verse 7). Paul is not referring just to an inner attitude in giving, as if a right disposition could trigger the right response from God. Rather, he is suggesting that to give grudgingly is a sign of not applying oneself to the work using the gift of love, only a poor imitation of it.

In sum, Paul says in verses 6–10 that in extending to the Jerusalem needy what the Corinthians have received in the form of financial gain, a sign of grace in itself, they will receive a greater measure of gifts. There is of course no sense of earning these rewards — and here our earlier analogies break down — for the believers can no more own divine grace than they can earn the reward of righteousness. Rather, the Corinthians' rewards will be a greater measure of grace, and the result of this grace, according to verse 8, is self-sufficiency. Self-sufficiency was an ideal popular among Stoic and Cynic philosophers. It represented the highest human achievement in that it was understood to be freedom from all external circumstances, especially unfavorable conditions like poverty, wealth, fortunes, calamities, even other people. Such a state came as a result of training one's inner disposition and attitude, so that at the end one need not rely on anything or anyone else but one's own accomplished self. Here Paul borrows the concept, but he also changes it to describe an ideal that depends on the grace of God. God freely grants to the person all gifts so that he or she can in turn use these gifts "for every good work" (verse 8). This Pauline ideal is also marked by self-sufficiency and mastery of surrounding circumstances and conditions, "in everything in every circumstance always" — but such a notion of sufficiency derives its fundamental import from the conviction that all virtues are gained not through self-discipline but as a result of God's granting of divine grace, not in isolation from but in the service of others. The spiritual person receives from God and builds up the body of Christ.

If this is right, then an investment — if one could call it that — of gifts we receive from God will yield more gifts. Paul is suggesting to his Corinthian readers that the collection for the Jerusalem poor is actually an excellent investment opportunity. For what they give away is money, but what they will receive in return is the very thing they prize the most — divine grace. In so doing, Paul re-prioritizes the values with which the Corinthians are familiar, grace and money, community and self-sufficiency, and invites them to examine them. Imperceptibly, Paul in verses 9–10 also questions the notion of absolute ownership of material goods. He reminds his readers that it is God who supplies all these material goods and private ownership is only derived ownership. Nevertheless, Paul does not diminish the significance of the material in order to prop up the spiritual; in the midst of urging the Corinthians to give bountifully to the collection effort, it would be foolish of him to belittle money. Instead, Paul sees money as a significant medium to express the concrete love one community has for another and the unity of the Christian body. In so doing, Paul invites his readers to revisit the hierarchy of values that informs their lives and their Christian existence.

All this Paul summarizes in the first half of verse 11, "In everything, you are being made rich for the purpose of every act of generosity." Grace is given for the purpose of reaping gifts, and likewise the gifts of riches are given for the sake of "generosity." Good work begets good work, and grace spawns further grace. If this seems somewhat circular and tautological, Paul quickly adds in the second half of verse 11 that the ultimate purpose of the collection and the exercise of gifts given to us as a result of divine grace is to render thanksgiving to God. While the relief project will undeniably supply the needs of the Jerusalem poor, it will also succeed in soliciting thanksgiving to God (verse 12). With this new theme, which is to occupy him till the end of chapter 9, Paul also speaks in a new tone. Instead of pleading with the Corinthians he now speaks with optimism and confidence, and instead of using the future tense he now shifts to the present. It is as if he is so convinced the collection will be a success that he is already counting on the inexorable result that will bring glory to God.

Paul is convinced that this anticipated glorification of God will happen on two fronts. On the side of the Corinthians, they will glorify God "because of the obedience" that is based on their faith and "because of the generosity of [their] sharing with them and with all" (verse 13). These two reasons for glorifying God are here delineated in parallel but are most likely to be understood as synonyms. All along, Paul's view of the collection is that it is more than a matter of money. In 8:5 he praises the Macedonians for having shared themselves, and in 8:8 he raises the collection as an occasion to test the genuineness of the Corinthians' love. In line with these interpretations of the collection, therefore, Paul sees the anticipated success of the Corinthian effort as a demonstration of their faith in the gospel and their obedience. Such concrete manifestation of faith and love — signs of divine grace — is the reason for glorifying God.

On the other side, Paul continues, "They with prayer on your behalf long for you" (verse 14). Following as it does verse 13, "your sharing with them and *with all*," "they" might be taken to mean all the churches who might serve as witnesses to the Corinthian undertaking. This is possible in light of the impending visit by Paul and by the Macedonians in 9:1–5. But it seems more likely that "they" refers primarily to the recipients of the gift: namely, the poor in Jerusalem. In that case, Paul expresses his supreme confidence in their favorable reception of the collection and in the bond that is to develop between gentile and Jewish churches as a consequence of the gift. He is so confident that he expresses their gratitude in advance. They will be thankful not just for the gift but more so for "the surpassing grace of God among you." Grace in this respect is the common experience between the different churches and is therefore the foundation for unity. By the same token, unity among different churches is the manifestation of grace. Fittingly, Paul ends the appeal with "Thanks (*charis*) be to God for his indescribable gift!" (verse 15).

Paul's optimism would later prove to be premature. In 2 Corinthians 12, Paul would bitterly complain that the Corinthians have misunderstood him and that they persisted in bringing up the same charge that he — through the emissary of Titus and "the brother" —might have taken advantage of them financially. This can only refer to the advance party Paul sent to Corinth for the collection mentioned in 8:16–9:5; "the brother" must be the unnamed "tested and eager brother" of 8:22 who came originally from Paul's party. From this we can be fairly certain that, at least up till the writing of chapters 10–13,[23] if the collection succeeded at all, it might not have garnered as much as Paul had hoped. By the time of the writing of Romans, Paul's last surviving letter, he reports that he had completed the collection among the "Macedonians and Achaians" (15:25–26). Paul must have made good on his promise of a "third visit" which he threatens to make in 2 Cor 12:14; 13:1. On this trip he succeeded, albeit to an uncertain degree, in soliciting some money for the collection. The order of presentation in Romans, "Macedonians and Achaians," leads one to think that the Corinthians never did meet the challenge Paul laid down for them in chapter 8 and that their final contribution was less than that of the Macedonians.

Towards the end of Romans, Paul asks the Roman believers, apprehensively, to join him in a prayer that "[he] be rescued from the unbelievers in Judea and that [his] ministry for Jerusalem be pleasing to the saints" (Rom 15:31). Gone is the confidence that the recipients of the collection will embrace the givers in a show of Christian unity on account of God's outpouring grace on both gentile and Jewish congregations. Gone is the expectation that as a result of the successful demonstration of faith and love all the churches will join together in singing praises and thanksgiving to God (2 Cor 9:12–14). From what we read in Acts —which gives readers no information on the collection whatsoever — Paul made that fateful last trip to Jerusalem where he was promptly arrested, tried, and sent to Rome. The collection did not make a difference in reconciling gentile and Jewish Christians; it did not even make it into Acts.

Nevertheless, these two chapters give us an answer to Paul's stake in the collection, which goes straight to the heart of his theology and mission. For him the collection is the perfect platform for all to actualize their faith, love, and all the other spiritual gifts into moral actions. The giving of such a significant commodity as money would challenge Christians to reexamine their hierarchy of values, to see if their wealth, possessions, and material gains would come under the control of the grace of God, or is the grace of God to be sold for a pittance. Such a moral challenge is not limited to the personal sphere, however; it goes hand in hand with Paul's theological and missionary agenda of unifying gentile and Jewish churches and of extending the grace of God to a large-scale, worldwide manifestation, to be witnessed by all. If the new creation is in process, if cosmic transformation is already taking place, if God is in the process of reconciling the world to God's self, then the visible sign of that new creation is the unity of the fractured Christian communities. And the collection is the perfect vehicle to bring that to a realization.[24] Even if Paul's dream was unfulfilled, the vision he left behind has become an enduring legacy of the church.

*Chapter 6*_____

Fool's Speech: 10:1–13:13

As we come to chapter 10, Paul's tone takes a drastic change. At the end of chapter 9, we saw Paul draw the collection letter to a close with an optimistic declaration that he was certain that the Corinthians would generously contribute to the relief effort for the Jerusalem poor, and that the Jewish churches would embrace the offering as a sign of God's grace and as a symbol of unity between Jewish and gentile congregations. His mood was so buoyed and his confidence so high that he triumphantly proclaimed, "Thanks be to God for his indescribable gift!" (9:15). Chapter 10, by contrast, begins with a triple self-referential emphasis: "It is *I myself, Paul*, who appeal to you...." The sense of anxiety and urgency conveyed by this utterance is matched only by its irony. He appeals to the Corinthians "through the meekness and gentleness of Christ" (10:1), which in light of the defensive posture throughout these proceedings reads less like an admission of humility than a ironic caricature of the Corinthian converts' attitude towards him. He continues in the next breath, "I who am humble in person with you but bold towards you in absence" (10:1), unfurling a bitter objection to the characterization that he is unimpressive, even lowly and contemptible, whenever he appears in person, but is brash and vociferous only when he does not meet them face to face. In hindsight, his letters are at least partly to blame. Paul quotes his detractors who evidently have said, "His letters are weighty and strong, but his presence in body is weak and his speech is unimpressive" (10:10). Paul admits that his oratorical skills are amateurish (11:6), but he refuses to concede anything. He assures his readers that he is powerfully equipped with the mighty weapons of God, "for the destruction of strongholds. We destroy reasoning and every haughtiness raised up against the knowledge of God, we take every thought captive for obedience to

Christ, and we stand ready to punish every disobedience when your obedience is complete" (10:4–6).

This is clearly a different Paul than the one we have seen thus far in 2 Corinthians, especially the confident and optimistic Paul of chapters 8 and 9. The Paul who defended his change of itinerary, for example, held out hopes for reconciliation and forgiveness. Even when deflecting charges against him, as when he was charged with vacillating, saying "Yes, yes" and "No, no" all at once (1:17–18), Paul did not confront the Corinthians but made only an indirect appeal by means of a parenthetical remark on the theological veracity of the gospel and on the true character of God (1:19–22). Here in chapters 10–13, Paul uses threats and warnings: "I warned before and I am warning now … those who have previously sinned and all the rest that when I come again, I will not be lenient" (13:2). He insists on imposing his apostolic authority: "I wrote these things in my absence, so that when present I would not have to act severely in accordance with the authority which the Lord gave me" (13:10; see also 10:8). Gone are the subtle theological arguments; instead, Paul turns to the blunt weapon of intimidation.

Not surprisingly, Paul's tactics towards his opponents are also radically different. The Paul of earlier chapters referred to his opponents only obliquely, if also pejoratively. He suggested that those who had received money for their service were "peddlers of the word of God" (2:17), but otherwise desisted from attacking them frontally. He alluded to their use of letters of recommendation, but only by way of objecting to the demand placed on him to produce similar documents (3:1–3). Other than indirect references such as these, he refrained from engaging his opponents directly or even mentioning their positions. Instead, he entered into a complex discourse on the new covenant (3:5–18). He did the same thing later in 5:12–13 where he again only alluded to the antics of his opponents, referring once more to their use of letters of recommendation but also to their penchant for ecstatic demonstrations. But again, he did not confront his opponents directly or respond to them; he only urged his readers to mend their fissured relationship by becoming reconciled to him (5:14–21). Paul's defensive strategy throughout chapters 1–9 was one of appealing to the Corinthians' theological judgment.

In the highly charged chapters 10–13 (a part of Letter D), however, Paul abandons the subtle approach. In this letter, he

refers to his opponents directly and openly, calling them sarcastically "super-apostles" (twice in 11:5; 12:11) and assailing
them in a series of invectives as "false apostles," "deceitful
workers," and finally, to cap it all off, as "ministers of Satan" (11:13-15). He accuses them of trespassing in his territory
(10:12-16). He makes an uncompromising comparison of himself to the super-apostles in his memorable "fool's speech" (11:1-
12:10) with the intent of forcing the Corinthians to choose
sides.

The differences between chapters 10-13 and the rest of 2 Corinthians are so pronounced and so pervasive that they cry out
for explanation. The best seems to be that these four chapters
belong to an altogether different letter. Such a conclusion would
also agree with what we have observed previously: namely, these
four chapters presuppose what has gone on before and therefore
must have been written afterward (see chapter 5). For example,
Paul in 12:17-18 answers the charge that he was defrauding the
Corinthians in the collection project indirectly through the col-
laboration of Titus and the unnamed brother. That is clearly
impossible unless the advance party headed up by Titus described in chapters 8-9 (especially 8:16-24) had already made
the trip to Corinth and that the collection effort had already
failed. Chapters 10-13 could not have been written at the same
time as the collection letter (Letter C) or, for that matter, the
conciliatory letter as a whole (Letter B, 1:1-2:13 and 7:5-16).
Moreover, in comparison with Letter A (2:14-7:4) — in which
Paul explicates the rich meanings of authentic ministry and its
consequences (see chapter 4) — chapters 10-13 are much more
polemical and final in tone. Paul in these chapters creates a crisis situation for the Corinthians: he confronts them by making
them decide between withdrawing themselves from his opponents and becoming reconciled with the apostle, or suffering the
consequence of a permanent break with him. Paul gives them no
other choice. After such an ultimatum, it is difficult to imagine
Paul going back to a subtle approach. In all likelihood, therefore, Paul was forced to write this polemical letter, after all his
other letters had failed to address the fast-deteriorating situation
in the church. This letter represents Paul's last-ditch effort to
salvage what relationship was left between himself and his new
congregation.

In spite of the urgency of the situation, Paul's basic rhetorical strategy remains the same as before. He continues to stress

his relationship to the Corinthian congregation. Sarcastic and vitriolic as he is in this letter, he continues to appeal to the Corinthians' senses and hope to mend their broken relationship. His techniques are different, his tone is harsher, his criticisms of his opponents are more direct and more severe, he threatens rather than cajoles, he uses ironic speeches rather than theological arguments; but he does all this within the larger context of trying to call the Corinthians back to him. What Paul aims at achieving here is basically no different from before, except now the choices are laid out in uncompromising terms. He posits a stark contrast, an unbridgeable gulf between himself and his opponents. When he calls his opponents "ministers of Satan" (11:15), he in effect declares to the Corinthians that there can be no middle ground between him and his detractors.

Paul Lays Down the Gauntlet:
10:1–16

10 ¹It is I myself, Paul, who appeal to you through the meekness and gentleness of Christ — I who am humble in person with you but bold toward you when I am absent. ²I ask that when I am present I need not be so boldly confident that I dare consider opposing those who consider us conducting ourselves in a fleshly manner. ³For though we conduct ourselves in the flesh, we do not fight in a fleshly manner, ⁴for the weapons of our battle are not fleshly but mighty through God for the destruction of strongholds. We destroy reasonings ⁵and every haughtiness raised up against the knowledge of God, we take every thought captive for the obedience to Christ, ⁶and we stand ready to punish every disobedience when your obedience is complete.

In this opening paragraph Paul confronts his readers with a choice between two mutually exclusive, antithetical warring camps. He does it, appropriately enough, using military language. Paul begins innocently with an appeal "through meekness and gentleness of Christ,"[1] but this is a setup for the second half of the verse, "I who am humble in person with you but

bold towards you in absence" (verse 1). Paul does not immediately elaborate on this contrast between "humble" and "bold,"
but his readers are only too aware of what is at stake. Behind
the statement is the charge, occasioned by the appearance of
itinerant preachers in Corinth, that Paul writes strong, powerful
letters to the congregation but in person he is rather ordinary
and undistinguished: "His letters... are weighty and strong, but
his presence in body is weak and his speech is unimpressive"
(verse 10). Paul's rhetorically sophisticated letters are probably
responsible for raising an unrealistic expectation that is bound
to be disappointed when compared to personal appearance. Paul
later admits to being unskilled in speech, being an amateur when
it comes to the craft of oration (see 11:6). Whether this admission of weakness is intended to be taken ironically or literally,
broaching this subject indicates at the very least that the Corinthians' do perceive Paul as an inferior speaker in comparison
with his rivals. By noting this charge at the outset, Paul makes
it known to his readers that he is about to confront them with
a crisis, a decision between his apostolic office and that of his
detractors.

Paul sharpens his focus on this crisis in the next verse, as
he uses the same humble-bold contrast to issue a threat to the
Corinthians. The sentence is convoluted but the basic sense is
clear: he hopes that he does not have to resort to denouncing
publicly his critics who thought him "conducting [himself]...
in a fleshly manner" (verse 2). These critics are in all likelihood
those he later sarcastically calls "super-apostles." They consider
Paul *fleshly*, presumably because they understand themselves to
be blessed with the power of the *Spirit*. They have superhuman
of glossolalia, ecstatic speeches, extravagant power, and other
miraculous feats; Paul by comparison must appear to them as
weak and dull — that is, unspiritual and fleshly.

Paul's answer to his critics is already implicitly given in
verse 1 but is now coordinated with verse 4. Though he might be
meek and gentle, his is "the meekness and gentleness *of Christ*"
(verse 1), which in reality conceals the mighty weapon of God
"for the destruction of strongholds" (verse 4). Here Paul recalls
his argument in 1 Corinthians 1:

> For the message about the cross is foolishness to those who
> are perishing, but to us who are being saved it is the *power
> of God*. For it is written, "I will destroy the wisdom of the

> wise, and the discernment of the discerning I will thwart"
> (1:18–19 NRSV).

> We proclaim Christ crucified, a stumbling block to Jews
> and foolishness to Gentiles, but to those who are the called,
> both Jews and Greeks, Christ the *power of God* and the
> *wisdom of God* (1:23–24 NRSV).

Paul will make the same point later: "You seek proof that Christ
speaks in me, who is not weak toward you but strong among
you. For he was crucified out of weakness but lives in the power
of God. For we ourselves are weak in him, but we will live
with him by the power of God — for you" (2 Cor 13:3–4).
The power of God is capable of destroying all human wisdom,
all "strongholds ... reasonings and every haughtiness raised up
against the knowledge of God" (10:4–5).

The first-century writer Philo used the term "stronghold"
to mean an argumentative edifice constructed out of empty
speeches and human reasonings which at the end diverts one
from honoring God.[2] It was the favorite technique of the
Sophists and flashy orators, according to Philo, to hide their
vacuous thoughts behind flowery words and trickeries. These
arguments may seem, on the surface, impervious to attacks, but
in reality are only empty talk that does not probe the reality
of God's true character. By using this same criticism, equating "strongholds" to "reasonings," Paul presents his opponents
as cunning orators and sophistic chatterers who have erected
an empty edifice that cannot withstand divine attack. Using
military language, he assures the Corinthians that he will assault the strongholds of his enemies, and he will be victorious.
The outcome of a confrontation between human sophistry and
divine power is predictable: "We take every thought captive
for obedience to Christ, and we stand ready to punish every
disobedience" (verses 5b–6a).

Some commentators have noted a seeming tension internal
to verse 6: How can Paul be ready "to punish every *disobedience*
when [the Corinthians'] *obedience* is complete"? If the Corinthians' obedience has become perfect, so goes the argument, there
would be nothing in the congregation to punish. Paul's polemics
in verses 2–5 are directed against "those who consider us conducting ourselves in a fleshly manner" (verse 2), in other words,
the super-apostles. "To punish every disobedience" (verse 6a) is
therefore part of the same polemics. It is the itinerant preachers,

outsiders to the community, who are the very representatives of disobedience. In this context calling the Corinthians to obedience means nothing short of distancing themselves from the disobedient ones.

With this, the battle lines are drawn. On one side are the flashy talkers prone to using eloquent words to persuade the world. On the other side stands Paul, a weak and unimpressive figure. But he makes clear that he stands for the power of God which comes through the meekness and gentleness of Christ. The Corinthians will now have to choose between these two camps.

Attacks on the Super-Apostles:
10:7–11:15

10 [7]Look at what is before you. If someone is confident that he belongs to Christ, let him be reminded of this:[3] Just as he belongs to Christ, so do we. [8]If I boast a little too much of our authority, which the Lord gave us to build you up and not to destroy you, I will not be ashamed — [9]lest I seem to be frightening you through my letters. [10]"His letters," they say, "are weighty and strong, but his presence in person[4] is weak and his speech is unimpressive." [11]Let such a person count on this: However we appear to be in word through our letters when we are away, we will be the same in deed when we are present in person.[5]

[12]For we dare not classify or compare ourselves with those who recommend themselves. When they measure themselves by themselves and compare themselves to themselves, they show no comprehension. [13]We, however, will not boast beyond our proper limits, but only in keeping with the territory[6] that God has apportioned to us as our territory — that is, to come as far as to you. [14]For we do not overextend ourselves when we reached you, for we came to you with the gospel of Christ. [15]We do not boast beyond limits, in the labors of others; but we have hope that, as your faith increases, our work may be greatly expanded among you — in accordance with our territory — [16]in order to preach the gospel in lands beyond you, not to boast about work already completed in territory of others. [17]"Let him who boasts boast in the Lord" [Jer 9:24]. [18]For the one approved is not the

one who recommends himself but the one whom the Lord recommends.

11 ¹O, would that you put up with my foolishness a little! But you do put up with me. ²I am zealous for you with a zeal of God, for I betrothed you to one man, to present you as a pure virgin to Christ. ³I fear lest somehow, as the serpent led Eve astray by his scheme, your thoughts may be enticed away from the sincere and pure devotion to Christ. ⁴For if someone who comes preaching a Jesus other than the one we preached, or if you receive another spirit than the one you received, or a different gospel from the one you received, you put up with the person easily enough.

⁵For I consider myself not in the least inferior to the super-apostles. ⁶Though I am an amateur in speech, I am not so in knowledge. Rather, in everything we have made this clear to you in all things. ⁷Did I commit a sin when I debased myself, so that you might be lifted up, because I preached the gospel to you free of charge? ⁸I have robbed other churches by taking payment from them for the sake of your ministry, ⁹and while I was with you and in need, I was a burden to no one, for the brothers coming from Macedonia supplied my needs. I strove and will strive to keep myself from being a burden to you in any way. ¹⁰As the truth of Christ is in me, this boast of mine will not be silenced in the regions of Achaia. ¹¹Why? Because I do not love you? God knows I do!

¹²That which I do I will continue to do, in order to cut off any claim by those who want an opportunity to be recognized as our equal through what they boast of. ¹³For such people are false apostles, deceitful workers, disguising themselves as apostles of Christ. ¹⁴And no wonder: for even Satan disguises himself as an angel of light. ¹⁵It is therefore no great surprise if his ministers also disguise themselves as ministers of righteousness, but their end will accord with their works.

Many commentators consider 10:7–11, some including even 10:12–18, as part of Paul's appeal to the Corinthians in the opening paragraph. But beginning with verse 7 (which refers to an unnamed "someone"), it is clear that Paul is turning his attention to his opponents and is beginning to distinguish himself sharply from them. The charge in verse 10 that Paul's letters are powerful while his bodily presence is humble is already hinted at in verse 2 and might indicate that verses 7–11 belong to the first part of chapter 10. But as we have seen, Paul alludes to that specific charge for the express purpose of emphasizing the paradoxical nature of God's power. The contrasting perceptions of him when he is present with the Corinthians and when he is absent from them bespeak God's mighty weapon that is concealed in Christ's lowliness. It is better therefore to take 10:7 as the beginning of Paul's polemics against the super-apostles.[7]

This letter is exceedingly difficult to divide into subsections, since one topic leads to the next. Paul's emotions in this letter are running so high, and his attacks on his opponents are so broad and deep, that he scarcely has any opportunity to stop to arrange his thoughts in a more logical pattern. It makes for difficult analysis, but in many ways entertaining reading. Consequently, it is best not to divide this letter into subunits — as we have done thus far in the book — so small that it would take away from the fluidity of Paul's prose or lessen the impact of his polemics. It seems for easier to arrange our discussion topically.

Paul's Refusal to Accept Financial Support

One of the most persistent problems in Paul's relation to the Corinthians was his refusal to accept money from them. It had become an issue already in 1 Cor 9:8–18. In 2 Corinthians, it probably does not help Paul's cause that while he insists on carrying on his ministry free of charge, his opponents are willing to accept money for their work.[8] Paul earlier alludes to this when he distinguished himself from his opponents, the "peddlers of God's words" (2:17). This most likely points to their receiving payments as part of their ministry among them, an action Paul characterizes in terms of street vendors plying their wares for financial gains. By stark contrast, Paul refuses Corinthian support, thereby also refusing to be their client. His explanation is that he is content to "preach the gospel free of charge" and not be a burden to the church (11:7–9; 12:13–16).

To make matters worse, Paul does accept money from other churches, especially the Macedonians (11:9), with whom the Corinthians are in competition for Paul's attention. Paul is not unaware of the competition; he even goes so far as to use the competition between these two congregations for the promotion of the Jerusalem collection (8:1–4; 9:2–4).[9] And here he particularly relishes telling the Corinthians that "the brothers

coming from Macedonia filled my needs" (11:8). But accepting
money from other churches was not how Paul supported himself primarily. In his letters in general, but particularly in the
Corinthian correspondence, Paul makes it known that he works
with his hands (1 Thess 2:9; 1 Cor 4:12; 2 Cor 6:5). Acts pre-
serves a tradition that Paul worked as a tentmaker to support
himself (Acts 18:3). A tentmaker was someone who worked using leather and canvas to make or repair shades, awnings, and
sailcoth.[10] This would put Paul in the artisan class, and it might
mean setting up a workshop in Corinth to sell his goods and service. But such manual work was roundly despised by the upper
class as demeaning and lowly. The young Cicero writing from
Athens takes note of such manual labor:

> In regard to trades and other means of livelihood, which
> ones are to be considered becoming to a gentleman and
> which ones are vulgar, we have been taught, in general,
> as follows: First, those means of livelihood are rejected as
> undesirable which incur people's ill-will, as those of tax-
> gatherers and usurers. Unbecoming to a gentleman, too,
> and *vulgar are the means of livelihood of all hired workmen*
> *whom we pay for mere manual labour, not for artistic skill;*
> *for in their case the very wages they receive is a pledge of*
> *their slavery*. Vulgar we must consider those also who buy
> from wholesale merchants to retail immediately; for they
> would get no profits without a great deal of downright
> lying; and verily there is no action that is meaner than mis-
> representation. *And all artisans are engaged in vulgar trades;*
> *for no workshop can have anything liberal about it*. Least re-
> spectable of all are those trades which cater to sensual
> pleasures: "Fish-mongers, butchers, cooks, and polterers
> and fishermen," as Terence says. Add to these, if you please,
> the perfumers, dancers, and the whole vaudeville crowd.
> But the professions in which either a higher degree of in-
> telligence is required or from which no small benefit to
> society is derived — medicine and architecture, for example,
> and teaching — these are proper for those to whose social
> position they are appropriate.[11]

This is probably what stands behind Paul's characterization of
himself with mocking exaggeration as "humble": "Did I commit
a sin when I *debase* myself, so that you might be lifted up...?"
(11:7). When the call for the Jerusalem collection come around

these quarters, all the adverse conditions seem ripe to spawn the suspicion that Paul only using the occasion to raise funds for his own ministry in an underhanded way. He makes the appearance of not relying on the church's support, so goes the charge, but he is really defrauding the congregation. It is against this charge that Paul stages a bitter defense in 12:17–18.

We can hazard a guess as to why Paul refused financial support from the Corinthians. The reason is not simply that Paul did not want to put any undue burden on the Corinthian church in order to build up the congregation, as he repeatedly claims in his letters. The Corinthians probably interpreted his offering such general sentiments as self-justification. That Paul had to give the same answer over and over again, both in these chapters and indeed throughout the entire Corinthian correspondence, would lead us to suspect that none of his self-defenses had ever succeeded in silencing the persistent murmuring among his critics. While there is no reason to doubt Paul's genuine affection for the church of Corinth, there is still ample room to speculate about his action in the context of first-century patron-client relationship. As we saw before, the Roman patron-client system, through which wealthy patrons contracted with any and all who could prove to be useful to his household, was the social system that stood as backbone to the early church (see chapters 2 and 4). The Corinthian congregation no doubt functioned in much the same way: patriarchs whose houses were used for the worship assembly would be in a position to determine the agenda or the church and would be understood, even expected, to have authority over all clients under their patronage. Paul's refusal to accept financial assistance from these wealthy patrons was tantamount to refusing to be a client to these powerful patrons.

One possible reason for this can be traced back to the social and economic inequalities of the Corinthian church. From 1 Corinthians, we are certain that the congregation was a mixture of members from the wealthier and poorer classes (see chapter 2). There were probably not many who belonged to the equestrian or aristocratic classes, as Paul acerbically says, "none of you are of the noble class" (1 Cor 1:26). Nevertheless, there must have been plenty of wealthy heads of households who could not find a place among the aristocratic elites but had amassed enough wealth to be significant patrons. At the same time, the church was also made up of people from the lower social and economic ranks in society. Much of the disagreement over eating meat (1 Corinthians 10), the Eucharist (1 Corinthians 11), perhaps even different sexual mores (1 Corinthians 7) could be traced to the different responses to these issues by members of different social classes. If Paul were to accept patronage from only a segment of this fractious community, he would surely further exacerbate this inequality and contribute to the division between the haves and the have-nots. And that, judged in light of Paul's constant refrain in 1 Corinthians that while all things are possible not all things are beneficial to the unity of the body of Christ, would be an intolerable situation.

A second reason for rebuffing the offer of patronage has to do with the conflict of power and authority between apostle and patron. While Paul had clear apostolic authority with his converts, the patron-client system would make the head of the household a powerful figure to reckon with. It was after all in his house where the worship assembly and Eucharistic rites would take place. It was under his financial umbrella that all the early church works were carried out. And it was the conversion of the patriarch that was the most effective means of evangelization, since his whole household — wife, children, slaves, clients, employees — would follow suit. Paul's first Corinthian converts likely belonged to this class. This type of authority conferred by the prevailing social system was sure to clash with the type of charismatic authority (1 Corinthians 12–14) which Paul claimed for his apostolic office.

We get a glimpse of these two competing forms of authority in conflict in Paul's letter to Philemon. Paul's superb rhetorical skills in this letter often mask the conflict of authority between a patriarch and an apostle that made them necessary in the first place. While he has the authority, says Paul, "*in Christ* to command" Philemon the patriarch "to do his duty," to take back the run-away slave Onesimus, yet he would rather appeal to him "on the basis of love" (Philem 8–9). But why would Paul leave such a life-and-death issue as the acceptance of a run-away slave to the vagueness of love? The answer is Paul had no choice in the matter. He had apostolic authority; he had earned it in the course of his ministry and through afflictions and sufferings which came as a result of preaching the gospel. He makes sure Philemon knows it by reminding him, "I, Paul, do this as an old man, and now also as a prisoner of Christ Jesus" (verse 9; see also verse 1). But Philemon had both civil and social authority. It was well within his legal rights to insist on punishment or absolution. Furthermore, he was the owner of the house in which the church was based, and was therefore its patron (verse 2). Judging from Paul's request for a room (verse 22), it is not inconceivable that Philemon was also in some way *his* patron as well. In lieu of a clear, unambiguous locus of authority, Paul could insist on his apostolic authority only to a limited extent; for the rest he would have to rely on his rhetoric.[12] If we can draw a conclusion from Philemon, Paul refused to submit to the patronage of the Corinthian church, probably because he wanted to preserve his apostolic freedom and authority. There is no evidence that Paul wanted to question the utility of the system, since he did accept money from other congregations and perhaps even from Philemon. But an acceptance of Corinthian sponsorship would represent a dilution of his clear-cut charismatic authority as an apostle.

Paul's accepting gifts from far-away Macedonian churches would not put him in such a problematic position. There is no evidence that the Macedonian churches were infected by the same inequality evident in their more cosmopolitan, more affluent counterparts in Corinth. The churches in both cities seemed to be more impoverished in general and their means more evenly distributed, even if they could still make substantial contributions to the Jerusalem relief effort, according to 2 Cor 8:2–3. They exhibited such unity and love for one another (see 1 Thess 1:7–8; 4:9–10; Phil 1:9) that for Paul to accept financial support from the congregation did not mean committing himself to one faction versus another. In any case, we read of Paul's acceptance of their assistance only when he was far away from them: He received support from "the brothers coming from Macedonia" (2 Cor 11:9) while he was in Corinth, and he received a gift from the Philippian congregation while in jail, most likely in Colossae (Phil 4:16–18). While he was still in the cities working with the congregations, he carried on his customary practice of working for a living: "You remember our labor and toil, brothers and sisters, we worked night and day, so that *we might not burden any of you* while we proclaimed to you the gospel of God" (1 Thess 2:9). In Thessalonica as in Corinth, Paul refused financial support from the congregation while he was working in their midst, in order to preserve his apostolic authority by not being subjected to a powerful patron.

Paul's Opponents

Paul's frontal assault on his opponents gives us for the first time direct statements about his opponents. Glimpses of them culled from Paul's more allusive statements in the earlier chapters can now be corroborated and assembled in a reasonably coherent picture. Paul's opponents evidently have made extensive use of recommendation letters from authority figures in the early church (3:1; 5:12), a practice to which Paul again refers here in 10:12. By contrast, Paul has no such letter to show and, as the founder of the Corinthian congregation, he should by all rights have no need to rely on this kind of instrument, because it is necessary only for outsiders. Paul made essentially the same argument in 3:1–4, and he reiterates it in 10:18: "approved is not he who recommends himself but the one whom the Lord recommends"; and again in 12:11: "For I should be recommended by you, since I was in no way inferior to the super-apostles."

But if these super-apostles have to rely on references to gain entry into the Corinthian church, they must have been itinerant preachers from the outside. Their outsider status is confirmed by Paul's criticisms of them in 10:12–18. Paul insists that he and his fellow-workers "will not boast *beyond limit* but in accordance with *the measure of the territory* (literally, "canon" or "rule") that the God of measure has apportioned to us — to come as far as even to you" (10:13). What Paul makes clear here is that the mission field has already been marked off into separate spheres or territories, and that each missionary is already assigned to his or her proper turf. He reiterates the point two verses later, "We do not boast beyond limit in someone else's labors" (verse 15a). He admits that he plans some day to expand beyond his present limit — to lands far beyond Corinth — but he reminds his readers of the rule governing the mission field which dictates that each worker cannot trespass into someone else's territory: "We have hope ... to be greatly extended through you beyond our territory, to preach the gospel into lands beyond you, not to boast in another territory for things that have been prepared" (verses 15b–16). All this is obviously said in criticism of the super-apostles, who are indeed outsiders laboring in others' — that is to say, Paul's — territories, boasting in Paul's labors, and reaping his fruits in his absence.

But who are these super-apostles? Where do they come from? On whose authority do they rely for recommendation? Paul's language in 10:13 gives us a clue. The mission field is supposed to be determined "in accordance with the measure of the territory that the God of measure has apportioned to us." Underlying such a statement is an assumption that there is a standard, a rule, by which these territories are finally and unambiguously assigned. The likeliest candidate for the establishment of such a rule is the Jerusalem Council mentioned in Galatians. Regardless of how others might have interpreted its results — and there is good reason to think that the opponents understood them differently — Paul takes them to mean a sharp division of jurisdiction between those ministering to gentiles and those ministering to the Jews. James, Peter, and John, the so-called "pillars," will continue to minister to the circumcised, while Paul will work among the uncircumcised (Gal 2:7–9). To Paul this means that those working in these two territories must honor the boundaries dividing them and never stray into someone else's assigned field. Paul sees this as a sacred rule, established by "the God of measure" no less, which he accuses the itinerant missionaries of having violated.

The comparison with Galatians is appropriate for another reason. Paul in 2 Corinthians represents himself as a father, presenting the Corinthians as a chaste virgin to be betrothed to Christ, but he is dismayed that these Corinthians have been misled by the tempter, just as Eve was enticed by the serpent (11:2–3). Behind such imagery is probably the well-known Jewish tradition that Eve's downfall was some kind of sexual perversion.[13] In using such a metaphor, then, Paul portrays the Corinthians' heeding of the super-apostles as unfaithfulness to Christ. "If he who comes preaching *a Jesus other than the one we preached*, or you receive another spirit than the one you received, or a different gospel from the one you received, you put up with him easily enough" (11:4). The references to "another Jesus" and a "different gospel" here are familiar to anyone who has read Galatians, where Paul lambastes the church for leaving the true gospel for "another gospel" (Gal 1:6): "If we or an angel from heaven preaches to you a different gospel from that one we preached to you, let him be anathema!" (Gal 1:8). For emphasis he repeats the same curse in the very next verse.

The use of the same terminology here cannot be accidental. Paul must be intending to warn the Corinthians of the same danger to which the Galatian church has fallen prey, and his opponents in 2 Corinthians must be the same group of Jewish

Christians who advocated a law-centered Christianity in Corinth just as they have tried to do in Galatia. This conclusion is further corroborated in 11:22, where Paul says sarcastically, "Are they Hebrews? So am I. Are they Israelites? So am I. Are they the seed of Abraham? So am I." Their ethnic identity most likely plays an important role in their effort at insinuating themselves into the midst of the Corinthians. They probably claim to be genuine Hebrews or Israelites, but more importantly "the seed of Abraham." These are the same issues that Paul deals with in Galatians as well, and his mention of them here can only mean that the same group of missionaries have followed his footsteps to Corinth and have made inroads into the congregation's heart and soul.

If that is the case, we can begin to understand why Paul is anxious to insist on the territorial integrity of the mission field in 10:12–18. In his mind, since the Jerusalem Council has already committed itself to distinguishing the Jewish mission from the gentile mission, these Jewish-Christian missionaries have no right to trespass into his workplace. That is why in Galatians he recounts the decision of the Jerusalem Council to his readers. Here, too, he brings up the decision again to show why these outsiders are trampling on someone else's field. By the same token, the most natural origin for the super-apostles' letters of recommendation is that they receive their backing from Jerusalem, since they likely consider it the mother church and Paul an inferior apostle. Any criticism of Paul would somehow be traced back to his apostolic credentials and stature. All this would explain Paul's hyperbolic sarcasm of calling these itinerant preachers "super-apostles" (11:5; 12:11). These, Paul warns, are "false apostles" (11:13), a name that recalls his designation of his rivals in the Jerusalem Council as "false brothers" (Gal 2:4).

In 2 Corinthians, we have a fuller picture of these Jewish Christian missionaries than in Galatians. Paul charges in 10:7 that "if someone is confident that he belongs to Christ, . . . so do we." The enigmatic expression "to belong to Christ" is puzzling, since it clearly does not mean the ordinary sense of "being in Christ," which defines the new life of every believer. It could imply a kind of special relationship to Christ the Spirit or, given the itinerant preachers' connection to Jerusalem, it could refer to their understanding that they are specially commissioned by Jesus. In Mark 9:41, Jesus says to the disciples, "Whoever gives you a cup of water to drink in my name because *you belong to Christ* ... will not lose his reward."[14] In implying that Paul has no such special commissioning, of course, the super-apostles are suggesting that Paul has no apostolic status and, therefore, he belongs to an inferior class of missionaries. In response to this sensitive charge, Paul refers them to answers he has given before, in 1 Corinthians, that he too has seen the risen Lord and that he too has been commissioned by Christ to carry out the ministry (see 1 Cor 9:1; 15:8–10).[15]

It appears, then, that the super-apostles have consistently compared themselves to Paul, a practice Paul mocks in 10:12, "We dare not classify or compare ourselves with those who recommend themselves." Comparing oneself with important teachers and authority figures was a standard way of enhancing one's prestige during Hellenistic times.[16] The super-apostles are evidently known to be engaged in it, and subsequently compare themselves favorably to Paul (see 11:12). They are the ones who suggest that when Paul is away from Corinth, he is powerful in his letters, but is actually weak in person (10:1–2, 10). They probably judge Paul to be unsophisticated in the art of oratory (10:10; 11:6), which may indicate they consider themselves to be accomplished speakers. They probably also claim that their special spiritual power grants them a commanding presence, attended by ecstatic experiences (5:13; 12:1–4) and by "signs, wonder, and miracles" (12:12).

Paul can of course try to match the super-apostles' claims, and at times he does in fact do that: "I consider myself not in the least inferior to the super-apostles" (11:5); he repeats the same statement in 12:11 and again later in the fool's speech (11:22–23). But such a strategy is freighted with dangerous consequences. Even if Paul could conceive of winning such a debate, the terms of the debate would make a mockery of Paul's principle of preaching Christ crucified. The power of God shows through the weakness of the cross, and divine wisdom shines through the foolishness of a suffering Messiah dying a slave's death. A comparative strategy, on the other hand, is designed to crown the triumphant winner on the basis of human strength and wisdom — precisely the opposite of what Paul has been preaching all along.

Under these circumstances, Paul adopts a strategy of not trying to win the debate but changing the terms in which the debate is ordinarily carried out. The old debate privileges strength over weakness, but Paul strenuously argues that human weakness must be the mark of an authentic minister because, as he has shown in his discussion of clay vessels in 4:7–15, human frailty demonstrates the power of God. In other words, if he wishes to change the terms of the debate, he must demonstrate the futility of comparison by showing not how strong he is but how weak he is. The intent of such a strategy is to tear down the notion of superiority itself and to subvert the common dependency on a comparative game to add to one's worth. The only way to do that is, paradoxically, to lose the debate. To defeat the argumentation of the wise, the sophistry of the crafty, he must speak like a fool.[17]

The Fool's Speech:
11:16–12:13

11 [16]Again I say, let no one think me a fool. But even if you do, receive me like a fool, so that I might also boast a little. [17]What I speak I speak not by the Lord but as a fool, in this business of boasting. [18]Since many boast according to the flesh, I too will boast. [19]For gladly you who are wise put up with fools, [20]for you put up with it when someone enslaves you, when someone devours you, when someone takes you in, when someone puts on airs, when someone strikes you in the face. [21]To my shame I say this as if we were weak.

[21]In whatever thing anyone might be bold — I speak in foolishness — in that too I am bold. [22]Are they Hebrews? So am I. Are they Israelites? So am I. Are they seed of Abraham? So am I. [23]Are they ministers of Christ? — I am speaking like a madman — I am more: with more labors, with more prisons, with far more blows, often near death. [24]Five times I received from the Jews forty strokes minus one, [25]three times I was beaten with a rod, once I was stoned, three times I have been shipwrecked, for a night and day I was in the depths of water; [26]often on journeys, in dangers from rivers, in dangers from robbers, in dangers from kinsfolk, in dangers from the gentiles, in dangers in cities, in dangers in the wilderness, in dangers at sea, in dangers among false brothers; [27]in labor and hardship, in wakefulness often, in hunger and in thirst, often without food, in coldness and nakedness; [28]not to mention the pressure on me every day, from anxiety for all the churches. [29]Who

is weak and I am not weak? Who is tripped and I am not burning with indignation?

30If I must boast, I will boast of the things related to my weaknesses. 31God and the Father of Lord Jesus — blessed is he forever — knows that I do not lie. 32In Damascus the Ethnarch under King Areta guarded the city of Damascus in order to seize me, 33and through a window I was let down in a basket through the wall and I escaped his hands.

12 1It is necessary to boast. It is not profitable, but I will go into visions and revelations of the Lord. 2I know a man in Christ who fourteen years ago — whether in the body I do not know or out of the body I do not know, God knows — was caught up to the third heaven. 3And I know that such a man — whether in the body or out of the body I do not know, God knows — 4was caught up to Paradise and heard unutterable words which no mortal is permitted to speak. 5On behalf of such a man I will boast; on behalf of myself, however, I will not boast, except of weaknesses. 6For if I want to boast, I will not be a fool, for I am speaking the truth. I refrain, lest someone might regard me higher than that which one sees in or hears from me, 7even considering the surpassing character of the revelations.

Therefore, in order that I might not be over-elated, a thorn in the flesh was given to me, a messenger of Satan to beat me, so that I might not be over-elated. 8I asked the Lord three times about it, that it leave me. 9And he said to me, "My grace is sufficient for you, for power is made perfect in weakness." Thus I will more happily boast in my weaknesses, that the power of Christ may rest upon me. 10Therefore I take delight in weaknesses, in insults, in needs, in persecutions and calamities — for Christ's sake — for when I am weak, then I am powerful.

11I have become foolish; you made me do it. I should be commended by you, for I was in no way inferior to the super-apostles, even though I am nothing. 12The signs of the apostle have been performed among you with all patience, by signs, wonders, and miracles. 13How have you been made inferior to the other churches, except that I did not burden you? Forgive me this wrong!

After announcing that he would speak like a fool in 11:1, Paul takes the circuitous route by means of attacking the super-apostles (verses 2–15) before reminding his readers in verse 16 that he will indeed begin a fool's speech. The speech itself is based on the well-honed technique of comparison (Greek, *synkrisis*), the very technique that Paul accuses his opponents of using (10:12). It was a literary convention to highlight the uniqueness of one thing over against another or, in the case of the opponents, to enhance their own reputation and prestige by comparing themselves to other apostles. Paul willingly plunges into this exercise, at least initially, but his real intent is to subvert the logic of comparison altogether.

Paul introduces the speech by first making clear that he is drawn into boasting by others who do so "in the flesh" (11:18): He speaks not on the authority of the Lord but in a worldly manner like a fool (11:17). The word for "foolishness" here (Greek, *aphrosynē*) is different from the "foolishness" of 1 Cor 1:18 (Greek, *mōria*). The latter connotes dim-wittedness, the former incoherence and senselessness. Paul later uses "madman" (Greek, *paraphronōn*) in 11:23, which is someone who speaks or acts contrary to reason or sensibleness. Paul's point here, therefore, is not the same as in 1 Corinthians 1, that God's foolishness is wiser than human wisdom; he does not even purport to speak on behalf of the Lord. Rather, Paul announces that he enters into the comparison, not as a sane person but as one without sense or logic, one who has no coherence or reason. If the conventional wisdom in a comparative competition is to prove one's virtues, merits, or intellect, then Paul lets on that he intends to play the exact opposite role. If the goal is to win the match, Paul's express goal is to lose the match. What Paul aims at doing in his fool's speech is to set up a reverse comparison, so that he will emerge in defeat! Only such a radical rhetorical surgery could excise the competitive cancer that is growing in the minds of his readers.

To let his readers know that this is exactly what he is about to do, Paul prefaces his speech with a sobering observation on how the Corinthians have in fact been victims of the opponents' comparison game without ever realizing it (verses 19–20). Thinking they are wise themselves, the Corinthians have in reality been mistreated by the super-apostles. "Someone enslaves you, devours you, takes you in, puts on airs, strikes you in the face" (11:20) describes how these self-important ministers, armed with the superiority given to them by the logic of comparison, are destined to play the abuser in an unbalanced relationship. Under such circumstances, Paul would much rather plead, "We were weak" (11:21a).

The fool's speech proper begins in verse 21b, "In whatever thing anyone might be bold — I speak in foolishness — in that too I am bold." This determines the form of the comparison in the next verse and a half. This comparative structure can be best viewed with the following arrangement:

THE SUPER-APOSTLES VS. PAUL

Are they Hebrews?	So am I.
Are they Israelites?	So am I.
Are they the seeds of Abraham?	So am I (verse 22).
Are they servants of Christ?	I am more ... (verse 23a)

The first three titles — Hebrew, Israelite, seeds of Abraham — Paul has no trouble matching. Elsewhere, Paul has never been slow to acknowledge his ethnicity (see Gal 1:13–14; 1 Cor 9:20; Rom 9:1–5; 11:1; Phil 3:4–6). It is one area in which Paul refuses to suffer fools gladly. But with the title "servants of Christ," Paul begins his reverse comparison — with a litany of hardships and sufferings he experienced as a result of the ministry. We have encountered similar lists before, in 4:8–10 but especially in 6:4–10, except that the list here is much lengthier and delivered with more emotion. In 6:4–10, in particular, the enumerated hardships all serve to define the true character of the "ministers of God" (6:4), not only because human frailties paradoxically lift up the power of God, but also because sufferings form the basis of the authentic minister's identification — with the sufferings and death of Christ (see 4:11, 14). Paul most likely presupposes the same theological understanding here, but the recitation of hardships does something more. It serves to set up the punch line, "Who is weak and I am not weak? If I must boast, I will boast of the things related to my weaknesses" (verses 29–30). In sum, Paul begins his comparison with his opponents by matching them point for point, but he turns it all around by proving that he is after all weak, the exact opposite of his competitors. In the reverse logic of Paul's comparison, he can score points only by proving himself to be the exact opposite of his opponents.

As a last item in his fool's speech, Paul recalls an ecstatic experience to prove his point (12:1–10). As we saw in 5:13, the super-apostles must have had impressive displays of their spiritual power and their ecstatic demonstration. Paul alludes to their power even here. He says he is reluctantly to talk about his own spiritual experiences, "It is *not profitable*, but I will go into visions and revelations of the Lord" (12:1), with the clear implication that he is drawn into this by his competitors. Here Paul follows the same procedure as he has established earlier in chapter 11. He begins by suggesting that, like his opponents, he too has seen visions, but just as one enters the internal logic of such a comparison, he turns it upside down by showing that his ecstatic vision demonstrates precisely the opposite: namely, he is but a weakling, someone who is helplessly dependent on God's grace.

The vision itself is a rare first-century account of a vision reported in the first person. Paul at first maintains the literary fiction of speaking of himself as the visionary in the third person, "I know a man..." twice (verses 2, 3), even going so far as drawing a distinction between himself and the visionary, "On behalf of such a man I will boast; on behalf of myself, however, I will not boast, except of weaknesses" (verse 5). But he lets this distinction drop in verse 7, "... in order that *I* might not be over-exalted," and continues the rest of the narrative in the first person singular. The reason for the distinction is purely rhetorical. Since he has already established the principle that weakness is the preferred term of the debate, it would make a mockery of his new logic if he were to adduce this experience to prove his power. He is nevertheless recounting the experience, not only to give his Corinthian readers a not-so-subtle reminder that he, too, has extraordinary power, but also to drive home the conclusion of the narrative which will demonstrate paradoxically his weaknesses.

To be granted an entry into Paradise is the highest mystical experience in some first-century Jewish circles. Though some Jewish traditions would identify Paradise with the seventh and highest heaven, it is equally common to find traditions that would posit only three heavens. In any case, Paul's point here is obviously not that he made it only midway to the highest heaven but that he achieved what few people even dream of: namely, the entrance into Paradise itself (verse 4). It is an out-of-body experience, "Whether in the body I do not know or out of the body I do not know, God knows" (verses 2, 3), and Paul is told things that no other mortals are allowed to utter (verse 4).

But the main point of the narrative lies not in the first half but in the second (verses 7b–10). Paul says that he would have significant grounds to boast of this ecstatic experience, and the secret revelations he heard would automatically grant him a status higher than anyone else. This he freely admits in verse 6. But the narrative is a rhetorical setup, because he immediately tells his readers that he was given the famous "thorn" in his flesh — in order to keep him from becoming over-elated (verse 7b). No amount of scholarly research or debate will ever be able to reveal what the thorn is. Paul gives his readers no clue as to what it might be. The word used here means literally "stake," the kind used for defense or impalement. It is evidently a blow delivered by an angel of Satan. But there is no way of telling whether Paul means it literally or figuratively, or whether it is something external to himself or internal. Whatever it might be, the point of mentioning the "thorn" is that at the height of his mystical achievement, he is reminded that the real source of power is not human achievement but God. The saying in verse 9, "My grace is sufficient for you," is reported here as direct revelation, which seems to heighten the irony: the content of the vision is further revelation, but it reveals that revelation is unimportant. This, then, symbolizes the Paradise narrative and provides a fitting conclusion to the fool's speech. The point of the ecstatic experience is that the experience itself not a sign of his special power; but only that "power is made perfect in weakness" (verse 9). "Thus I will more happily boast in my weaknesses, that the power of Christ may dwell upon me. Therefore I take delight in weakness, in insults, in needs, in persecutions and pressures for Christ's sake, for when I am weak, I am powerful" (verse 10). Ecstatic experience turns out to be self-emptying and self-relativizing.

The short epilogue to the fool's speech in 12:11–13 serves as a recapitulation of all the major themes that have gone on before. The Corinthians make Paul launch the fool's speech: he should be recommended by them; he is in no way inferior to the super-apostles; signs and wonders have been performed in the Corinthian congregation; he has not accepted money from the Corinthians because he does not wish to burden them. But the epilogue also provides a transition to what follows in 12:14, which is preparation for a third visit.

Preparation for Visit as Direct Warning:
12:14–13:10

14Look, I am prepared to come to you this third time, and I will not be a burden, for I do not seek what is yours, but you yourselves. For children do not need to store up for their parents but the parents for the children. **15**I myself will most gladly spend and be exhausted for you. If I love you exceedingly, am I to be loved less? **16**Granted, I myself did not burden you, but "Being cunning, I took you by deceit"? **17**I haven't taken advantage of you through anyone I sent you, have I? **18**I appealed to Titus and sent the brother along: Titus didn't take advantage of you, did he? Didn't we walk in the same spirit and take the same steps?

19All along you were thinking that we were defending ourselves before you. We are speaking in the presence of God, in Christ: All things, beloved, are for building you up. **20**For I fear that somehow if I come I would find you not to be what I wish and you would find me to be not what you wish; that somehow there may be strife, jealousy, anger, disputes, evil slander, gossip, pride, unruliness; **21**that if I come again God would humble me before you and I would weep for many of those who have previously sinned and have not repented of their uncleanliness, immorality, and licentiousness they practiced.

13 **1**This is the third time I am coming to you; "Upon the mouth of two or three witnesses will every announcement be substantiated" [Deut 19:15]. **2**I have issued warnings while I was present with you in my second visit, and I am issuing warnings now that I am away, to those who have continued in their sinful ways and all the rest: when I come again, I will not be lenient — **3**since you seek proof that Christ speaks in me; he is not weak towards you but strong among you. **4**For he was crucified out of weakness, but he lives by the power of God. We ourselves are weak in him, but we will live with him by the power of God — for you.

5Test yourselves to see if you are in the faith and prove yourselves: Do you truly know that Jesus Christ is in you? Unless you fail the test! **6**I hope you will know that we ourselves have not failed the test. **7**We pray to God that you do no evil, not so that we might appear to have passed, but so that you do good, even though we might be shown to have failed. **8**For we can do nothing against the truth but only on behalf of the truth. **9**For we rejoice when we are weak and you are powerful; for this also we pray — building you up. **10**Therefore, I write these things while I am away, so that when I am present I would not have to act severely in accordance with the authority the Lord gave me — for building up, not for destruction.

Several obstacles stand in the way of his third visit. The obvious one is what Letter D is primarily designed to overcome: namely, to wean the Corinthians of outside missionaries who have been seducing them from Paul. But there is another one — the matter of money. We have already seen how Paul refuses financial assistance from the Corinthians in order to maintain his apostolic freedom and authority. Paul now adds an additional concern: some members of the Corinthian congregation must have attributed Paul's refusal to accept money *and* his rigorous pursuit of the collection project for the Jerusalem church to his "being cunning" and full of deceit (12:16). This is perhaps entirely understandable, since it is not unlikely that some members found Paul to be inconsistent when he refused money on one hand and asked for it on the other. All this no doubt contributed to a general distrust of Paul's motives and character. From the rhetorical questions Paul poses for the Corinthians, "Titus didn't take advantage of you, did he? Didn't we walk in the same spirit and take the same steps?" (12:18), we can surmise that Titus and his companions must have failed to convince the Corinthians to complete the collection, and that the root cause for this set back was the suspicion that Paul and company might be defrauding the church. The collection for the poor in Jerusalem, as we will see below, eventually did come to some satisfactory conclusion during his "third visit," when Paul succeeded in finally settling his differences with the Corinthian church. For the time being, he still must deal with the Corinthians' lingering suspicion that his motives for the collection were less than honorable.

Paul answers this problem by reiterating his customary practice of not burdening his congregations when he makes his third visit: "I will not be a burden" (12:14). Given the general context, Paul seems to be implying that when he makes his visit he will support himself by working while he sojourns in the city of Corinth. This juxtaposition of Paul's impending visit and financial independence creates an allusive reference to how he supported himself, without burdening anyone in the church, in his founding visit. This action of his he has already described earlier using the exact same language: "while I was with you and in need, I was a burden to no one" (11:9). The recollection of his founding visit, in turn, is designed to prompt the Corinthians to remember Paul's general character while he was with them. He therefore can legitimately tell his readers that he is their loving and devoted father who spends all he has exhaustively for the sake his children (12:14–15). Paul tries to make clear to the suspicious church that his main concern is not himself or what he could gain from the Corinthians, but the Corinthians themselves: "I do not seek what is yours, but you yourselves" (12:14). All this is indicative of his excessive love for the Corinthians; but if so, Paul poses a question to the Corinthians, is it fair that his love is now repaid with suspicion: "If I love you exceedingly, am I to be loved less?" (12:15).

We recall that Paul's refusal to accept money has been derided as a sign of a deficient apostleship by his enemies, but here Paul turns this criticism to his favor. If he has never received money for his ministry among the Corinthians, what would cause the Corinthians to suspect that he might begin now? To remain suspicious of Paul, one would have to conclude, is simply illogical.

There also appear to be another set of issues that stand in the way of Paul's third visit, and these have to do with some wrongdoings — "sinful ways" (13:2) — of which the Corinthians have yet to repent and which are still being perpetuated (13:2).[18] These "sinful ways" could be somehow related to the "uncleanness, immorality, and licentiousness" described in 12:21, or the "strife, jealousy, anger, disputes, evil slander, gossip, pride, unruliness" of 12:20. What exactly are entailed by these lists is not immediately clear. It is possible that these two lists refer to concrete acts, but it is far more likely that they are meant to be general lists of vices similar to the ones found elsewhere in Paul's letters (for example, Gal 5:19–21). In the last analysis, what these sinful ways are is probably far less important than how Paul uses them to his advantage.

In a perverse way, these wrongdoings have strengthened Paul's hand in his struggles with his enemies for the hearts and minds of the Corinthians, since these wrongdoings actually create an opportunity for Paul to exercise his apostolic authority.

We can see this by comparing the two mentions of his impending visit in this passage. While the first announcement in 12:14 is immediately followed by a series of defensive comments (12:15–18), the second announcement of the same visit is 13:1 is set in the context of the Corinthians' vices (12:20–21) and Paul's impending judgment against the wrongdoers (13:2–3). This enables Paul to assert himself: "I have issued warnings while I was present with you in my second visit, and I am issuing warnings now that I am away, to those who have continued to sin and all the rest: when I come again, I will not be lenient" (13:2). This no doubt puts the Corinthians on the defensive, even as Paul gains the upper hand by asserting his apostolic authority.

Thus, Paul concludes the letter with a series of admonitions to the Corinthians in 13:5–9. All the admonitions revolve around the test of authentication: "Test yourselves to see if you are in the faith and prove yourselves: Do you truly know yourselves that Jesus Christ is in you?" (13:5). Regardless of what they think of Paul or of his enemies, the singular test that matters to the Corinthians ought to be whether "Jesus Christ is in you." Whether Paul is finally shown to have passed or failed the test, is a matter of indifference to him. He expresses this in the rather confusing verse 7: "We pray to God that you do no evil, not so that we might appear to have passed, but so that you do good, even though we might be shown to have failed." There is no logical relation between "you do no evil" and "not so that we might appear to have passed," just as there is no connection between "you do good" and "even though we might be shown to have failed." What Paul wants to convey is the overall effect that the Corinthians' doing good or evil is a separate matter from Paul's being right or wrong. Contentions and struggles on the question of apostolic legitimacy might seem, in the heat of the battle, like the all-consuming passion that they appear to be. But all that pales in importance when compared to the Corinthians' own life in Christ. That is why, Paul says, he does not mind being weak, so long as the Corinthians are powerful (13:9). The messenger cannot usurp the supremacy of the message. Paul and all other missionaries only serve "on behalf of the truth" but cannot go "against the truth" (13:8).

The letter ends with a final recapitulation of the whole letter, a *précis* of Paul's aim, in verse 10: "Therefore, I write these things while I am away, so that when I am present I would not have to act severely in accordance with the authority the Lord

gave me — for building up, not for destruction." This last verse
harks back to the beginning of chapter 10 where Paul is accused
of being humble in the presence of the Corinthians but strong
only in his absence (verse 1). He now answers that accusation
with a thunderclap: he in fact has full authority to be powerful, to be severe in person. But be careful what you wish for!
The Corinthians may indeed receive the strong, powerful apostolic presence that they wish for, but in the hands of Paul, that
powerful presence could well be used for punishment.

Some commentators have suggested that "third visit" refers
to the third visit since the founding visit (making a total of
four visits). But it seems more reasonable to suppose that Paul is
here referring to his third visit overall (which makes the founding visit his first), especially in view of his statement that he
had warned the Corinthians of their sins "while I was present
with you in my second visit" (13:2). According to 2 Cor 2:1 and
7:2,[19] Paul made a second visit to Corinth, an unexpected visit
resulting in his being humiliated by a member of the church,
which he later would call a "painful visit." That confrontational
visit would seem to fit the general atmosphere of threats and
warnings described in 13:2.

The third visit probably came off better than Paul had anticipated. Paul's letter to the Romans in all likelihood was written
from Corinth during this time (see Rom 16:1, 23; compare with
1 Cor 1:14). In Rom 15:25–26, Paul reports that the collection
from the Greek churches has now been completed, and that he is
ready to accompany it in person to Jerusalem: "Now I am going
to Jerusalem ministering the saints. For Macedonia and Achaia
were pleased to share their resources with the poor among the
saints in Jerusalem." "Achaia" here undoubtedly includes Corinth, the unrivaled leading city of the province. In spite of much
wrangling and infighting, then, it appears that Paul's visit did
somehow succeed in stilling the Corinthians' disquieting suspicion of his motives behind the collection and he was able to
persuade the church to contribute to it. There is no indication
in Romans how this was done, but contribute to the collection
the Corinthians clearly did. The total sum collected from the
church of Corinth, however, must not have been as generous as
Paul had hoped for coming from such a wealthy city as Corinth.
By the way he lists Achaia after Macedonia in Rom 15:26, the
total contribution of the Macedonians must have been greater

that that of the Corinthians. Nevertheless, all this points to the plausible likelihood that the stormy situation in the church had calmed down to allow Paul to finish the collection project and to provide enough respite for him to compose his most systematic, most subtly argued treatise, his letter to the Romans. We can only imagine that his last letter to the Corinthian church had accomplished some salutary effect.

At the same time, in Romans Paul writes that he plans to go to Spain after he delivers the offering to the Jerusalem church. In fact, Romans has been composed with the purpose of convincing the church in Rome to become a new partner in his western mission to Spain:

> Now with no further place for me in these regions [that is, in Asia Minor and the provinces around the Aegean Sea like Macedonia and Achaia], I desire to come to you when I go to Spain. For I do hope to see you on my journey and to be sent on[20] by you [that is, to be supported by you in my missionary efforts] once I have enjoyed your company for a little while (15:23-24 NRSV; see also verse 28).

If so, this represents a departure from his original missionary plan mentioned in 2 Cor 10:15-16: "we have hope that, as your faith increases, that our work may be greatly expanded among you — in accordance with our territory — in order to preach the gospel in lands beyond you." Paul must have, at one point in his ministry, planned to establish at Corinth a base of operation for new missionary activities to the western Mediterranean world. Since Corinth was such an advantageous convergent point for all sea and land routes north and south, that was an eminently sound strategy. But the report in Romans would lead us to suspect that Paul had a change of plan. He now would rather set up his new center in Rome. All this would lead us to speculate that during the extensive stay of his third visit to Corinth, he must have come to realize that his relationship with the Corinthians had been so irreparably damaged that the city could hold no future for him and his missionary enterprises. As Paul was already casting about for a new missionary center — *while* he is still living in Corinth (under Gaius's patronage; see Rom 16:23). His relationship to the Corinthian church must have been cool and detached at best. We hear no more mention of Corinth after this, and it seems certain that after his departure from the city Paul severed his relationship with the church once and for all.

Final Benediction:
13:11–13

13 [11]Finally, brothers and sisters, farewell, be in good health, be consoled, be mindful of the same things, be peaceful, and may the God of love and peace be with you. [12]Greet each other with a holy kiss. All the saints greet you. [13]The grace of the Lord Jesus Christ, the love of God, and the fellowship of the Holy Spirit be with you all.

The final benediction is stereotypical in many ways since it resembles many other closing benedictions in Paul's letters. But it is unclear if these three verses represent the ending of chapters 10–13 or of the whole of 2 Corinthians which is a composite. If the latter, they could represent a reworking by the later editor who stitched 2 Corinthians into its present form.

A surprising element, however, is the fully trinitarian formulation of verse 13, which has nothing comparable in the whole of the Pauline corpus. Its mention of the "grace of the Lord," "the love of God," and "the fellowship of the Holy Spirit" recalls the baptismal formula of Matt 28:20, but unlike the latter it does not mention Christ as "Son" and God as "Father." It therefore does not actually posit any specific relationship between the three persons. It is well within Paul's theology to compose such a benediction.

Notes

Chapter 1: Introduction

1. For example, Romans and 1 Thessalonians, though neither is completely devoid of polemical statements.

2. See chapter 5 for a detailed discussion of the collection.

3. It should be pointed out that the theory presented here and assumed throughout the book is one of many. Some have proposed that 2 Corinthians is not a composite of different letters but a unitary whole (so Philip E. Hughes, *Paul's Second Epistle to the Corinthians* [Grand Rapids: Eerdmans, 1962], xxi–xxxv). This theory, in my view, cannot stand up to scrutiny and has been rejected by most commentators. Victor Furnish proposes a moderate view, taking chapters 1–9 as constituting a single letter and chapters 10–13 to be a different letter; see his *II Corinthians* (Garden City: Doubleday, 1984), 35–41. Some have claimed to have detected as many as seven letters. The position taken in this work is similar to that of Dieter Georgi ("Corinthians, Second Letter to the," *Interpreters' Dictionary of the Bible Supplement* [1976], 183–86), except that I take chapters 8–9 to be a single letter and I do not take chapters 10–13 to be the so-called "letter of tears."

4. The event is also recorded in Acts 18:1–18.

5. For a more detailed portrait of these itinerant preachers, see the discussion of 2 Corinthians 10–13 in chapter 6.

6. Such a lengthy stay would have also required substantial resources at his disposal, resources which would likely have been supplied by Gaius, in whose house Paul was staying (Rom 16:23).

7. For a chronology of Paul in general and the Corinthian correspondence in particular, see relevant sections in Jerome Murphy-O'Connor, *Paul: A Critical Life* (Oxford: Clarendon, 1996). Murphy-O'Connor is in broad agreement with Robert Jewett, *Dating Paul's Life* (London: SCM, 1979).

8. For the relationship between scripture and the community of faith, see W. C. Smith, *What Is Scripture? A Comparative Approach* (Minneapolis: Fortress, 1993).

9. Marcel makes a distinction between a precritical reading (first *naïveté*) and a post-critical reading (second *naïveté*). According to the first *naïveté* fascination with the text is based on an ignorance of the problems in the text, a fascination which criticism can easily desta-bilize. In the second *naïveté*, however, fascination comes *in spite of* and perhaps even *because of* criticism. Thus, the relationship between reader and text is renewed and reestablished. See his "La piété selon Peter Wust," in *Etre et Avoir* (Paris: Fernand Aubier, 1935) 319–57, for his discussion on the "first" and "second *naïveté*."

10. David Tracy, *The Analogical Imagination: Christian Theology and the Culture of Pluralism* (New York: Crossroad, 1981), 115–16.

11. So, for example, Albert Schweitzer, *The Mysticism of Paul the Apostle* (London: A. & C. Black, 1931).

12. The term "kenotic" comes from *kenosis* ("emptiness"), which the author of the Philippian Hymn (Phil 5:6–11) uses to characterize Christ's divestment of the "form of God": "But he *emptied* himself, taking on the form of a servant" (verse 7).

Chapter 2: The Civic and Social Context of Second Corinthians

1. Suggested, persuasively, by John Chow, *Patronage and Power: A Study of Social Networks in Corinth* (JSNT Supplement 75; Sheffield: JSOT Press, 1992) 38–82.

2. So Pausanius *Description of Greece* 7:16.7–10. It is only fair to assume that Pausanias, writing around the third quarter of the sec-ond century C.E., depended on a source for his information on the devastation of Greek Corinth by the Romans. A less complete but ear-lier account of the fall of Corinth can be found in Strabo *Geography* 8.6.23a–23b, who depended on the eyewitness account of Polybius (203–120 B.C.E.). For biographical information of Strabo, see note 7 below.

3. Whether Corinth was in fact the capital of Achaia is open to question, though the evidence, circumstantial though it is, points ir-resistibly in that direction. All of Greece had been under the supreme command of the governor of Macedonia prior to 27 B.C.E., at which point Achaia was separated from Macedonia and declared a senatorial province (Strabo *Geography* 17.3.25). In 15 C.E., Tiberius incorporated Achaia into the imperial province of Moesia (Tacitus *Annals* 1.80.1), but Claudius returned the province to the control of the senate (Suetonius *Claudius* 35.3), at which point Corinth was likely to have been estab-lished as its capital. See Victor P. Furnish, *II Corinthians* (Anchor Bible; Garden City: Doubleday, 1984), 9.

4. The Isthmian games came under Corinthian sponsorship once again probably some time between 7 B.C.E. and 3 C.E.

5. Along with Patrae and Athens, so according to Plutarch *De vi-tando aere alieno* 7 (*Moralia* 831A). Plutarch's description actually puts Corinth at the top of the list. See interpretation of this passage in Murphy-O'Connor, *St. Paul's Corinth*, 105.

6. Many of these building projects were sponsored by freedmen; see J. H. Kent, ed., *Corinth VIII 3: The Inscriptions 1926–50* (Princeton: ASCSA, 1966). For the significance of this, see below.

7. Strabo was born around 64 or 63 B.C.E. and died 21 or 22 C.E. According to his own account, he traveled to Corinth a number of times, the latest of which was probably 29 B.C.E. His *Geography*, where the following quote is found, was based partly on his personal travel and partly on works of previous geographers he found in the library of Alexandria. The work was completed around 7 B.C.E. and slightly revised in 18 C.E., that is, roughly the same time of Paul's sojourn in the great city. See Jerome Murphy-O'Connor, *St. Paul's Corinth: Texts and Archaeology* (Wilmington: Michael Glazier, 1983), 51–52. See 8.6.22a for his description of the two harbors of Corinth at Lechaeum and Cenchreae.

8. A promontory at the southeastern corner of the Peloponnese known, at least in literary tradition from Homer down to Byzantine times, for its sudden change of winds and its danger.

9. Cited in Murphy-O'Connor, *St. Paul's Corinth*, 53–54.

10. So Murphy-O'Connor, *St. Paul's Corinth*, 14.

11. Found in Murphy-O'Connor, *St. Paul's Corinth*, 14–15.

12. See Murphy-O'Connor, *St. Paul's Corinth*, 56, for more references.

13. Murphy-O'Connor, *St. Paul's Corinth*, 68.

14. See the summary and bibliography on the debate whether Corinthian bronze was being made in Corinth in the first half of the first century in Ben Witherington, *Conflict and Community in Corinth: A Socio-Rhetorical Commentary on 1 and 2 Corinthians* (Grand Rapids: Eerdmans; Carlisle: Paternoster, 1995), 10 n. 23.

15. See J. W. Hayes, "Roman Pottery from the South Stoa at Corinth," *Hesperia* 42 (1973), 416–70.

16. *Geography* 8.6.23c.

17. There is evidence, however, that Corinth did not lie empty after its total devastation in 146 B.C.E. Nevertheless, squatters could not have produced the kind of highly prized bronze of which Plutarch and Pliny spoke so fondly.

18. Plutarch *Lives* Caesar 47.8.

19. As indicated before, Corinth was most likely never left devoid of inhabitants for the century or so after its destruction. But the local would obviously occupy a lower social class when the colonizers came in.

20. Found in Murphy-O'Connor, *St. Paul's Corinth*, 51.

21. Murphy-O'Connor, *St. Paul's Corinth*, 113.

22. See the study of mobility in first-century urban centers, of which Corinth was a prime example, in Wayne Meeks, *The First Urban Christians: The Social World of the Apostle Paul* (New Haven: Yale University Press, 1983), 16–23.

23. See Meeks, *First Urban Christians,* 51–73.

24. Meeks, *First Urban Christians,* 51–53. Here Meeks draws on and critiques works by E. A. Judge, A. Deissmann, and Gerd Theissen.

25. This gives us a hint of Paul's missionary strategy as well. He evidently evangelized those who had the means to provide a basic foundation for his communities before he founded the church.

26. See Archibald Robertson and Alfred Plummer, *First Epistle of St. Paul to the Corinthians* (2d ed.; International Critical Commentary; Edinburgh: T. & T. Clark, 1914), 396 note. This observation is largely supported by Gordon Fee, *The First Epistle to the Corinthians* (New International Commentary on the New Testament; Grand Rapids: Eerdmans, 1987), 831–32.

27. So Meeks, *First Urban Christians,* 58. This is not impossible but it would assume that the Corinthians used such yardsticks as social standing and wealth to determine status.

28. See Gerd Theissen, *The Social Setting of Pauline Christianity: Essays on Corinth* (Philadelphia: Fortress, 1982), 57, 92–94; Meeks, *First Urban Christians,* 59.

29. See Meeks, *First Urban Christians,* 59.

30. Murphy-O'Connor, *St. Paul's Corinth,* 37.

31. Theissen, *Social Setting,* 75–83; Furnish, *II Corinthians,* 25.

32. So Henry Cadbury, "Erastus of Corinth," *Journal of Biblical Literature* 50 (1931), 42–58.

33. See Chow, *Patronage and Power,* 92–93, depending partly on P. R. C. Weaver, "Social Mobility in the Early Roman Empire: The Evidence of the Imperial Freedmen and Slaves," *Past and Present* 37 (1967), 3–20. See also Witherington (*Conflict and Community in Corinth,* 8), who reports numerous plaques, monuments, and inscriptions dedicated to public works that had been sponsored by slaves and freedpersons.

34. Meeks, *First Urban Christians,* 92.

35. See C. E. B. Cranfield, *The Epistle to the Romans II* (International Critical Commentary; Edinburgh: T. &. T. Clark, 1979), 783.

36. Chow, *Patronage and Power,* 101.

37. According to Abraham J. Malherbe, *Social Aspects of Early Christianity* (Philadelphia: Fortress, 1983), 98, Paul did not automatically confer authority on someone because of his or her wealth.

38. Slightly adapted from Chow, *Patronage and Power,* 30–33.

39. According to Ronald Hock, *The Social Context of Paul's Ministry* (Philadelphia: Fortress, 1980), 52–59. Acceptance of money was a major source of income for first-century sophists.

40. Chow, *Patronage and Power,* 109–10.

Chapter 3: A Letter of Reconciliation

1. In ancient epistolary theories, playing up the common history between the writer and readers in order to manipulate the latter into the desired position was an integral element of a friendship letter.

2. See chapter 2 for a longer discussion of the situation reflected in 1 Corinthians 9.

3. An apostle was therefore a figure of authority in the early church, although it is unclear what constitutes the exact nature of apostleship. For details concerning the city of Corinth and the region of Achaia, see chapter 2. The reason for Paul's not accepting the Corinthians' support but the Macedonians', according to Murphy-O'Connor, *Paul: A Critical Life,* 306-307, is that Paul was far away from the Philippians in Corinth, and the Philippian gift represented a communal effort. The Corinthian assistance, by contrast, was contributed mainly by the wealthy patrons of the community. Accepting it would mean alienating the poorer members of the community.

4. Paul Schubert, *Form and Function of Paul's Letters,* 50.

5. See 4 Maccabees for the idea of righteous suffering having efficacious power.

6. Similar phrases appear in Col 1:24; 1 Pet 1:11; 4:13; 5:1, however.

7. See discussion of 4:7-15 in chapter 4.

8. This is perhaps the reason why Paul greatly expands this theme to include a number of other terms in all his letters (e.g., 1 Thess 2:19) but especially in the Corinthian correspondence: 2 Cor 1:15, "confidence"; 3:4, "confidence"; 3:12, "boldness"; 6:11, "frankly"; 8:22; 9:3; 10:2, "boldness"; also 1 Cor 9:15. See also the use of the synonym "conscience," which is understood to be the human capacity for self-judgment, in 1 Cor 8:7-13; 10:25-29; 2 Cor 4:2; 5:11; Rom 2:15; 9:1; 13:5.

9. Perhaps this is the reason Timothy is also named as co-sender of this letter; see 2 Cor 1:1.

10. The syntax of 1:17 is notoriously difficult. "Lightly," "according to the flesh," and " 'Yes, yes' and 'No, no' " are all ambiguous.

11. See chapter 2 for the relationship between financial support and the Roman patronage system.

12. Victor P. Furnish, *II Corinthians* (Anchor Bible; Garden City: Doubleday, 1984), 144-45.

13. For Paul referring to himself as the "father" of the Corinthians, see 1 Cor 4:14-15; see also 1 Thess. 2:11.

14. So Furnish, *II Corinthians,* 163-68.

15. In 7:4, affliction and consolation are thematically linked to 7:5-7. But the latter refer to specific events, whereas the former are general considerations.

16. This is a controversial point; see overview of the Corinthian chronology in chapter 1.

17. Scholars have called this the "apostolic parousia." See Robert Funk, "The Apostolic Parousia: Form and Significance," in *Christian History and Interpretation: FS John Knox* (Cambridge: Cambridge University Press UP, 1967).

18. One can even make a case that this is where Paul first begins his travelogue, continuing with the recounting of the canceled double visit in 1:16.

Chapter 4: The Characteristic of Authentic Ministry

1. *Antony* 84–86.

2. See the Hellenistic-Jewish writing of the first-century *Wisdom of Solomon.*

3. Paul here may also be building on Joel 2:11: "Numberless are those who obey his command. Truly the day of the Lord is great; terrible indeed —*who can endure it?*"

4. See chapter 2 for patron-client relations in Roman society.

5. The Codex Sinaiticus reads "your" here. But "our" has far better manuscript support and makes better sense of the imagery. Paul argues that he does not need any written recommendation. But if he does, the Corinthians themselves would be that letter, which Paul carries with himself. A letter of recommendation of course stays with the recommended at all times, as an introduction of the carrier to all other places. This is precisely Paul's point in verse 2. "Your" came into the text here most likely as a result of being assimilated to verse 3, which is usually taken to refer to the Corinthians' reception of the gospel.

6. See Stanley B. Marrow, "*Parrhesia* and the New Testament," *Catholic Biblical Quarterly* 44 (1980), 431–46.

7. In other words, Paul is not making a trinitarian statement in 3:17, as if he were equating God the Father with God the Spirit.

8. See Sze-kar Wan, "Charismatic Exegesis: Philo and Paul Compared," *Studia Philonica Annual* 6 (1994), 54–82.

9. Although it is also possible that Paul is here thinking of Isa 9:2.

10. Furnish, *II Corinthians*, 251.

11. For similar catalogues in other letters of Paul, see Rom 8:35, 38–39; 1 Cor 4:11–13; Phil 4:12.

12. Paul has discussed the parousia extensively with the Corinthians in 1 Corinthians 15, and it is something he expects them to grasp.

13. See chapter 3 for discussion of 1:3–7.

14. So, for example, Hughes, *Second Corinthians,* 200–201.

15. So, for example, Rudolf Bultmann, *Der zweit Brief an die korinther* (Göttingen: Vanderhoeck & Ruprecht, 1976), 157–58.

16. The Greek has no subject: it reads literally, "If anyone is in Christ, a new creation." The most natural way to supply the subject is, "*There is* a new creation," which conforms to the contextual sense of the verse as well.

17. For other passages on the new creation, see Gal 6:15; but also Eph 2:15; 2 Pet 3:13; Rev 21:1; for OT background, see Isa 43:18–19; 65:17; 66:22.

18. See Hans D. Betz, "2 Cor 6:14–7:1: An Anti-Pauline Fragment?" *Journal of Biblical Literature* 92 (1973), 88–108.

Chapter 5: The Collection for the Poor

1. See chapters 1 and 2 for background of collection and for its relationship to Roman patronage.

2. So according to Acts 15:1–5. Whether the episode mentioned in Gal 2:1–10 is the same as that of Acts 15, and whether Gal 2:10 refers to the collection for the Jerusalem church are both questioned by scholars. But evidence seems to warrant answering both questions in the affirmative.

3. See Joachim Jeremias, *Jerusalem in the Time of Jesus* (Philadelphia: Fortress, 1969).

4. The designation "the poor" in Gal 2:10, without qualification (e.g., "the poor *in Jerusalem*"), appears to indicate that it is a proper noun used by the Jerusalem church as a self-designation.

5. Regarding Paul's collection effort among the Galatians, we hear no hint in Paul's letter to them. But it is no doubt something that Paul feels is sufficiently well-known to his readers that he can simply mention it in 1 Cor 16:1 without elaboration.

6. For Paul's later changes of plan, see chapter 3.

7. It is unlikely that Titus was the person who started the collection, as a first reading of 2 Cor 8:6 might lead one to believe, because in 7:13–16 but especially in verse 14, Paul introduces Titus as if the latter had just made his first trip to Corinth. And if 1 Corinthians was written prior to that trip, as it must have been from our reconstructed chronology of the letters (see chapter 1), then clearly the Corinthians were well aware of the collection before they met Titus.

8. This is the same plan that Paul announces in 2 Cor 1:16, which is different from 1 Cor 16:4, where Paul is still undecided whether to accompany the collection to Jerusalem. Somewhere in between Paul evidently changed his mind.

9. Literally, "imploring us with much appeal."

10. Literally, "for grace and fellowship." "Grace" (NRSV, "privilege") translates the Greek *charis*.

11. "Generous gift" here is literally "grace" (Greek, *charis*).

12. As at end of verse 6, "generous gift" translates the Greek *charis*.

13. See notes on verses 6, 7.

14. "True desire" is literally "the desire to will."

15. Hans Dieter Betz, *2 Corinthians 8–9* (Philadelphia: Fortress 1985), interprets 8:1–5 as an *exordium*, an introduction to a rhetorical piece.

16. Paul does not mention his acceptance of money from the Macedonian congregations in the same way he does in 2 Cor 12:13, which leads one to think that at the writing of 1 Corinthians, the problem might not have been too serious. By the time he wrote 2 Corinthians 8–9, though, he must have been aware of the issue.

17. See Furnish, *II Corinthians*, 415, who depends on Hans Windisch, *Der zweite Korintherbrief* (9th ed.; Meyerkommentar; Göttingen: Vandenhoeck & Ruprecht, 1924), 248.

18. Furthermore, such an interpretation would have difficulty assessing to what extent verse 9 ("for") is an explanation of verse 8.

19. 9:1 is syntactically linked to 9:3 by the Greek construction *men ... de...*, and the two verses can be translated as "On the one hand, it is superfluous...; on the other hand, I sent the brothers..." Given the context, it seems best to translate it as "Though..., nevertheless," as I have done here.

20. In any case, as Furnish, *II Corinthians*, 425–26, has pointed out, the formula is not exactly the same. Elsewhere Paul has *peri de* ("Concerning..."); here Paul has *peri men gar* ("For on the one hand, concerning...").

21. Philo *On the Special Laws* 1:78; cited in Furnish, *II Corinthians*, 435.

22. See the Septuagint version of Prov 11:21, 24, 26, 30; Job 4:8; Sir 7:3; *Testament of Levi* 13:6. For fuller references, see Furnish, *II Corinthians*, 440.

23. As we will see in the next chapter, 2 Corinthians 10–13 most probably belong to a letter written at a time later than 2 Corinthians 8–9. See also chapter 1.

24. The Danish scholar Johannes Munck has suggested that the reason why Paul was so concerned with the collection was that by leading a contingent of gentile representatives to Jerusalem with the collection, the action might provoke jealousy among the Jews and hasten the return of Christ (see Rom 11:25); *Paul and the Salvation of Mankind* (Richmond: John Knox, 1959), 303–4 (see also Furnish, *II Corinthians*, 412). This is possibly Paul's motive behind Rom 15:22–27, but as early as the writing of 1 Cor 16:4, Paul was still uncertain whether he would accompany the collection to Jerusalem. There seems to be a change of mind for Paul by the time of 2 Cor 1:16, but he does not let on that this is still the case in 2 Corinthians 8–9. By contrast, he em-

phasizes the unity of the church and the concretization of love as fulfillment of it. This latter motive might lie more directly behind these two chapters.

Chapter Six: Fool's Speech

1. This is not a supposed life of Jesus (as some commentators claim) but in all likelihood a kenotic theology of the kind depicted in the Philippian Hymn (2:6–11); see Furnish.

2. *Confusion of Tongues,* 129; cited in Furnish, *II Corinthians,* 462.

3. Literally, "let him consider this in himself."

4. Literally, "in body."

5. Literally, "However we are in word through letters when absent, thus also we are in deed when present." The NRSV translation, "What we say by letter when absent, we will also do when present," is somewhat misleading; it places the emphasis on saying and doing, based on common contrast in Greek between "in word" and "in deed." Paul's comparison here appears to be between the perceptions of him when he is absent and when he is present.

6. A difficult phrase: literally, "the measure of territory (Greek, *canōn*)."

7. It would be different, however, if the unnamed persons in 10:1–11 (verse 2 "those"; verse 7 "someone"; verse 10 "they"; and verse 11 "such a person") turn out to be members of the Corinthian congregation, as some scholars maintain. In that case, Paul could be seen as answering internal charges against him in verses 1–11. But the use of the third person in all these cases, especially verse 10, in contradistinction to the second person plural throughout this passage with which Paul addresses the Corinthians, would argue against this view. It is better to see the unnamed persons as the itinerant preachers against whom Paul devotes the next chapter and a half denouncing.

8. Ronald Hock, *The Social Context of Paul's Ministry* (Philadelphia: Fortress, 1980), 52–59, concludes that in the first century, there were four types of work with which an itinerant preacher could support himself: working for a living, attaching himself to a large household, begging, and charging a fee. The first two are familiar to us in the Corinthian correspondence. For more on this see chapter 2.

9. Paul's canceled double visit in 1:15 might also be related to this. See chapter 3.

10. Pliny the Elder even described an association of tentmakers. See citation and related activities connected with tentmaking in Jerome Murphy-O'Connor, *Paul: A Critical Life,* 86–88.

11. *De officiis* 150–51; cited in Murphy-O'Connor, *Critical Life,* 89; emphasis added by Murphy-O'Connor.

12. As well as on witnesses. Paul names as many as eight people (see verses 2, 23–24) in addition to the whole church which meets in Philemon's house. No doubt they serve as witnesses to the letters and to what action Philemon might take with Onesimus.

13. Victor P. Furnish, *II Corinthians,* 487.

14. By making this comparison with a saying in Mark, however, one does not have to subscribe to the theory that Paul's opponents came out of the Markan circle. It is enough to make it clear that they knew of Markan traditions.

15. This presentation of the super-apostles in all fairness is controversial. Cf., e.g., Murphy-O'Connor's hypothesis that Paul is steering between two competing groups in 2 Corinthians, the Judaizers and Spirit-people. The former are to be identified with the Judaizers of Galatians; the latter with the pneumatics in 1 Corinthians; see Murphy-O'Connor, "*Pneumatikoi* and Judaizers in 2 Cor. 2:14–4:6," *Australian Biblical Review* 34 (1986), 42–58. Dieter Georgi, on the other hand, suggests that the opponents are Hellenistic-Jewish missionaries; see *The Opponents of Paul in Second Corinthians* (Philadelphia: Fortress, 1986). Scott Hafemann, *Suffering and Ministry in the Spirit: Paul's Defense of His Ministry in II Corinthians 2:14–3:3* (Grand Rapids: Eerdmans, 1990), 147–148, argues that the "super-apostles" (11:5; 12:11) are to be distinguished from the "false apostle," "deceitful workers," and "servants of Satan" (11:13–15), and cites Käsemann, Bultmann, and Barrett for support; but Margaret Thrall ("Super-Apostles, Servants of Christ, and Servants of Satan," *Journal for the Study of the New Testament* 6 [1980], 42–57) argues that all three epithets are meant to be applied to the same group of people. See Furnish, *II Corinthians,* 48–54, for further discussion.

16. For references see Furnish, *II Corinthians,* 469.

17. There is a certain Zen-like quality to this mode of argumentation, according to which, using the technique of *kongan* (Japanese, *koan*), one could use what appears superficially as nonsensical sayings or stories to disrupt the normal expectation of logic or intuition. The end result is a questioning of normalcy and logic itself. One becomes illogical in order to usher in a new level of awareness.

18. This seems to be indicated by the perfect tense of *proēmartēkosi,* which implies a formerly sinful way being continued even now.

19. See the chronology laid out in chapter 1.

20. "To send on" (Greek, *propempein*) is likely a technical term among first-century early Christian missionaries. Paul uses it also in 2 Cor 1:16 to describe his wish to be "sent on" to Jerusalem with the collection from the Corinthians.

Index of Ancient Sources

2 Corinthians (continued)

General Index

Achaia, 7, 17, 32, 71, 103, 112, 113, 115, 123, 130, 132, 152, 153, 156, 159
  churches in, 52
Achaian League, 17
Achaicus, 24
aedile, 24–25
Aegean Sea, 42
affliction, 34, 35–38
aphrosynē, 144
apostolic apologia, 34
apostolic parousia, 160
Aquila, 24–25
Arabia, 33
Aristophanes, 19
arrabōn, 65
arrangement of letters, 6
Asia, 54
Augustus, 58

Barrett, C. K., 164
Beroea, 102, 104
Betz, Hans Dieter, 161, 162
blessing, 31–32, 34–36, 39, 44, 45, 54
brothers, unnamed, 8, 113–17, 123, 127, 133
Bultmann, Rudolf, 160, 164

Cadbury, Henry, 158
canon, 163
catalogue of hardships, 5, 35, 78, 79, 93–96
Cenchreae, 18
charis, 106, 107, 118, 161, 162
charisma, 106–8, 118
Chloe, 24, 25, 102
  people of, 24
chōrein, 92

Chow, John, 26, 156, 158
Christ-mysticism, 14
chronology of Paul, 155
Cicero, 134
Claudius, 156
Cleopatra, 58
clients. *See* patronage
collection, 4, 7–10, 17, 29, 34, 42–44, 56, 94, 96, 99–119, 121–27, 133–34, 149–50, 152–53, 155, 161, 162, 164
  as blessing, 106
  as contribution, 106
  as fellowship, 106
  as grace, 106, 108
  as ministry, 106
  as service, 106
  as sharing, 106
consolation, 34, 35–38
contextual dislocation, 4–5, 91–92, 97, 111–13, 126
Corinth, city of, 16, 17–21, 156–59
  ancient, 17
  as banking center, 18
  wealthy, 17
Corinthian bronze, 20, 157
Cranfield, C. E. B., 158
Crispus, 23, 24

Damascus, 33, 143
Deissmann, Adolf, 158
diakonia, 106
diakonoun, 106
double visit, 160

Ephesus, 8, 24, 35, 42
equality, 104, 110–11, 113
Erastus, 24, 25

Sze-kar Wan is Associate Professor of New Testament at Andover Newton Theological School in Newton Centre, Massachusetts.